LOCOMOTION PAPERS

THE RISHWORTH BRANCH

by
Jeffrey N. Fisher

THE OAKWOOD PRESS

© Oakwood Press 1990

ISBN 0 85361 391 5

Typeset by Gem Publishing Company, Brightwell, Wallingford, Oxfordshire.

Printed by Alphaprint, Witney, Oxford.

Bibliography

The following sources have been consulted in the preparation of this book:

The Lancashire and Yorkshire Railway, Volumes 1, 2 and 3: John Marshall
LMS Branch Lines 1945–1965: C.J. Gammell
The Rishworth Branch: The Lancashire and Yorkshire Railway Society
The Railway Magazine (March 1955): "The Rishworth Branch" by R.A. Cook
Bradshaw's Railway Guides
The Halifax Guardian
Halifax Evening Courier
Newsletters of the Lancashire and Yorkshire Railway Society
Railway through Calderdale 1840: E. Webster
The Railway Modeller
Files at the Public Record Office, Kew
Old Calderdale in Pictures: Down Memory Lane: E. Riley and R. Hardcastle
Ordnance Survey maps
The History of Ripponden: J.H. Priestley
Ryburn Tapestry: Hazel M. Whiteley
Ripponden Official Guide 1981
Report of the Calderdale Chief Town Planning Officer to the Development
    Services Committee: "Re-use of Disused Railway Lines for Cycle Routes"
    (1982)

Published by
The OAKWOOD PRESS
P.O. Box 122, Headington, Oxford.

Contents

A railmotor leaving Scar Head tunnel for Rishworth station. The 'up' line was the only one in use, the branch being worked as a single track. The 'down' line was occasionally used for storage of carriages.   *W. Kirkham Collection*

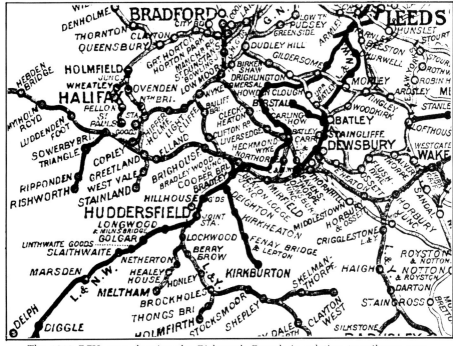

The 1913 RCH map showing the Rishworth Branch in relation to railways near Halifax.

Gradient Profile of the Rishworth Branch.

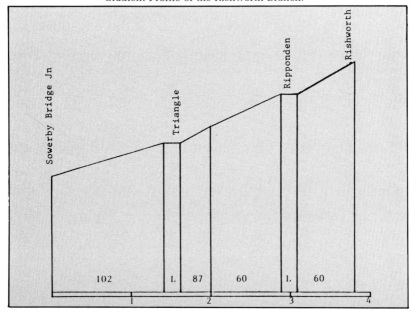

Introduction

During the second half of the nineteenth century the construction of railway branch lines proliferated throughout the country. These were lines serving communities away from the main through routes, which had either been geographically unsuited to the construction of a main line, or the population was such that it did not warrant this type of development.

Although, in terms of history, it has been a very short timescale since that period, so many changes have occurred in modes of transport that it becomes very difficult to imagine the impact the prospects of a new railway could have upon a community, and the excitement which developed as the project came to fruition. Up to this period relatively short journeys could only be undertaken with some trepidation, and it was not uncommon for people to live the whole of their lives without venturing more than a few miles from their home village.

This book examines the development of such a railway, the Rishworth branch in the West Riding of Yorkshire, and, seeks to convey the feelings prevalent in the villages served at the time of its inception and construction.

The Rishworth Railway has no particular claim to fame, it appears to have been first thought of as far back as 1845, been forgotten, resurrected in 1865 in a slightly modified form, opened for part of its length in 1878, opened throughout in 1881, and closed to passengers in 1929. Partial closure occurred in 1952, with total closure in 1958 and the line was dismantled about 1960. It is the very ordinary nature of the branch line which makes it an ideal subject for this book, and into the story and its effect on the social and industrial life of the Ryburn Valley can be read the story behind a great many similar ventures throughout the length and breadth of the country.

The Railway commenced at the small West Riding town of Sowerby Bridge, 2½ miles west of Halifax, and served directly the villages of Triangle, Ripponden and Rishworth in its 3.86 mile journey up the Ryburn Valley, a journey taking only 13 minutes. A further village, Barkisland, was served indirectly, with Ripponden Station subsequently being renamed Ripponden and Barkisland, whilst a halt called Watson Crossing, located between Sowerby Bridge and Triangle, was opened in 1907.

Jeffrey N. Fisher
1989

An old 'turn of the century' view of Sowerby Bridge station taken from an old postcard. *Oakwood Collection*

Map of the Rishworth branch, showing projected lines. *Courtesy, Railway Magazine*

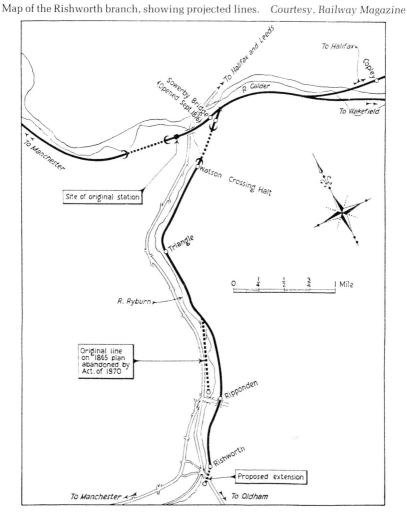

Chapter One
General Description of the Area

Rishworth and Ripponden are situated in the West Riding of Yorkshire in the parish of Halifax, and in the valley of the River Ryburn. Rishworth (or Rushworth) derives its name from the quantities of rushes which were prevalent within its boundaries or which were stored there, the word "worth" meaning a barn or a place of storage. It is not so easy to determine the derivation of Ripponden, but it is probable that it is formed from the River Ryburn, or Ryborne, as it was written in ancient deeds. Rhe signifies a river, and Rhy means a ford. Borne is a river, and dan, dene or den is a Teutonic word for a deep wooded valley. Rhy, or Rhi, also denoted a king in the ancient language of this country, almost as if the valley through which the Ryburn flows was, on some account, a royal dale, although this is something which cannot be accurately determined. A local historian called Watson, however, claimed he had seen the name in a very ancient document written as "Ryburghe", which signifies "the king's borough" or "station". It is possible that some king camped in the area with his forces in Saxon times as there is a large hill overlooking the village called Coney Garth, which is from the Anglo-Saxon cynig, a king, and the British, garth, mountain; i.e. the king's mountain.

Although the village itself is small Rishworth covers a significant area being 6,548 acres in extent. The majority of this, however, is moorland. There is very little level ground in the district and there is clear evidence to show that it was once well wooded. By and large the quality of the land is not good in agricultural terms, the bulk of it being used for the grazing of sheep. Lime can only be obtained from some distance away which, prior to the development of communications, made it a necessarily expensive commodity. There are significant quantities of good quality sand stone to be obtained in the district.

The River Ryburn was well stocked with fish prior to the establishment of paper mills in the upper reaches of the valley. The river has been prone to flooding from time to time with the earliest definite record being 18th May, 1722. This event damaged the church in Ripponden to such an extent that it was necessary to build a completely new one shortly afterwards. It is reported the graves were washed open and coffins forced out, with one being lodged in a tree some considerable distance away. No loss of life was noted but two instances have occurred since that date which did have such a result. Early one morning in November 1866, a newly married woman and three children aged 16, 14 and 11 were attempting to cross a wooden bridge on their way to work, when it broke in the centre and all were drowned. On 26th November, 1881 a Mr Kenworthy, together with his wife and daughter, were drowned in attempting to cross the river at night with their horse and cart when returning from Halifax.

There is no doubt that until comparatively recent times travelling about the district was very difficult. A certain John Taylor in his book called *News from Hell, Hull and Halifax* tells the reader "that on leaving Halifax he rode over such wayes as were passed comparison or amending, for when he went downe the lofty mountain called Blackstone Edge he thought himself in the land of Break-Neck it was so steep and tedious."

A general view of Ripponden and Barkisland station and goods shed.

R. Dyson Collection

Prior to 1758 communication throughout the country was very bad. In this particular area all goods had to be carried on pack horses as the roads were too narrow for wheeled vehicles and were in a dreadful condition. By an Act of Parliament passed in 1766 the narrow and rutted highways were to be replaced by macadamised roads, so called from their Scottish inventor McAdam. By this Act the leading gentry of Lancashire and Yorkshire were empowered to act as trustees to a major road in the area, and as this was adapted to the requirements of stage waggons and coaches, toll bars were placed at intervals to collect taxes to pay for the road. This trust was one of the oldest in the country. The tolls on this road were discontinued on 1st November, 1873.

It is very difficult to get any positive ideas of the level of population in very early times. In the days of the Normans and up to the middle of the last century, Rishworth was mainly an agricultural area which means that the population of necessity would be relatively low. There is little indication as to what extent this part of the West Riding was de-populated by the ravages of war, and especially the massacre by William the Conqueror, but the Domesday Book describes this part of the country as "waste".

The poll tax returns of Richard II give the earliest and most accurate information of population. At that time every person over 21 years of age who was not a beggar was taxed. If the number of persons in each township who paid the tax is multiplied by five it is possible to tell approximately the population at that time. Unfortunately for detailed comparison with the present day, the figures for Rishworth are combined with those for the adjoining district of Norland, the figure being 140.

From 1000 to 1764 A.D. is a long interval in the record and one which would have seen many changes, but it is not until 1764 that it is possible to again gauge the level of population. This information comes from the records of the then Vicar of Halifax and is based once again on allowing five people per family. The approximate population of Rishworth at that time was 645 people in 129 families; there were 131 houses, two of these being vacant.

By comparison the following figures were taken from official records which began on 10th March, 1801:

Rishworth   houses – 73 empty – 12 families – 159
            males – 518 females – 442 persons – 960

Although this is the official record it is considered that some mistake was made when looking at the number of inhabited houses compared with the number of families.

The following census returns showed the fluctuations in population during the last century:

Rishworth   1801 – 960, 1821 – 1588, 1841 – 1683, 1861 – 1244, 1881 – 1110,
            1891 – 982, 1901 – 915
The number of inhabited houses was 1831 – 253, 1891 – 189, 1901 – 189.

So far as trade and manufacturing industry is concerned the sparse population of the neighbourhood meant that agriculture formed the main pursuit. Initially each family tended to provide their own necessities with the labour being divided between the spinning and weaving of the wool from their own flocks, the care of the sheep and the growing of corn etc. A few corn mills were built to facilitate the grinding of the corn.

As time passed certain districts began to specialise in certain trades, particularly as the hilly nature of the land was not well suited to agriculture and it was only possible to grow enough corn for home consumption. More and more time was devoted by the local population to the weaving of cloth and ultimately the area became noted for this industry.

A large hall was built in Halifax, known as the Piece Hall, or Manufacturers' Hall, and was opened with considerable ceremony on New Years' Day 1779. It was used for the sale and display of "pieces" or lengths of woollen and worsted cloth. There had been other halls prior to this one used for the selling of cloth, Halifax probably being the first town in this country to erect a hall specifically for this purpose, the earliest mention of such being recorded in 1572.

The land for the construction of the Piece Hall was given as a gift by a local merchant, John Caygill (1708–1787). It was a fine building, constructed in a rectangular manner surrounding a courtyard some 10,000 sq.yds in size. The architects adopted the principle of Roman classical architecture. There were 315 rooms, and the manufacturer would display his goods in one of these. John Caygill gave a donation of £840 towards the construction of the building, and each manufacturer who contributed £28 4s. became owner of one of the 315 rooms. The total cost of construction was £10,000. By 1860 use of the building had declined and in 1868 it was sold to Halifax Corporation.

Under Corporation ownership the Hall experienced a variety of uses and gradually deteriorated in condition. In 1972 the Department of the Environment listed the Piece Hall as a Grade One property of historical and architectural interest. Shortly after this date it was agreed to restore the Piece Hall to its former glory. The official re-opening subsequently took place on 3rd July, 1976.

The building now houses an Industrial Textile Museum, Art Gallery, Tourist Information Centre with many of the individual rooms being used as shops. An open air market is staged in the courtyard on two days per week and various entertainments are staged there throughout the year.

A number of fulling mills and corn mills were erected on the Ryburn as early as the 16th and 17th centuries to provide the increasing population with work. It is recorded that in 1730 a Don Manuel Gonzales, formerly a merchant at Lisburn, made a voyage to England and he speaks of the importance of Halifax in the reign of Queen Elizabeth as follows:

> If such was the character and condition of the place then, what must it be since the great demand for kerseys to clothe the troops abroad. It is remarked that this Halifax and neighbouring towns are all so employed in the woollen manufacture, that they scarce sew more corn than will keep their poultry, and they feed very few sheep and oxen.

At this time there was a considerable manufacture of kerseys in the valley from Sowerby Bridge to Ripponden, these being purchased by merchants from Leeds and other places and forwarded to Hamburg and Holland. The whole of the British navy were said to be clothed from this source. As

Ripponden and Barkisland station looking towards Sowerby Bridge. A railmotor is seen at the platform with an 0–6–0 goods on the 'up' line. The goods shed can be seen on the right of the picture, behind the station.

R. Dyson Collection

A 2−4−2T locomotive running bunker first seen here with two coaches approaching Watson Crossing.This formation was used when the usual railmotor was not available. *R. Dyson Collection*

A poor photograph but one that shows Watson's Mills from the Sowerby Bridge side. The crossing can just be seen on the left. *R. Dyson Collection*

Rishworth was somewhat away from the main populated areas it was to a certain extent an exception to the development outlined above. Hand looms did come into this district however, this being explained in the following extract of a description of Halifax by an author called Pennant:

> The manufacture is far from being confined to the neighbourhood. The great manufacturers give out a stock of wool to the artificers, who return it again in yarn or cloth, but many manufacturers taking in a larger quantity of work than they can finish, are obliged to advance farther into the country in search of more hands which causes trade to spread from place to place.

The hand loom was a common article of furniture up to almost the middle of the 19th century, with nearly all the wool being combed at home.

In the latter part of the 18th century and the beginning of the 19th century mills began to be erected on the banks of the river, all of which were worked by water power. One of the largest water wheels on record was installed at a Rishworth mill as late as 1865. The cotton trade also began to grow about this time and many mills which had worked wool changed to cotton. Until about 1850 this became the staple industry of the valley.

In 1842 self-acting twiners came in to fill the place of hand twiners, and the first that were made were put in at Messrs Wheelwrights Mill, Rishworth. The silk industry was also introduced early in the 19th century.

With the increasing demand for paper a few of the mills were adapted to the manufacture of this commodity. Clean water was an essential factor and consequently such mills were located at the head of the river; due to the use of chemicals the fish stocks in the river were destroyed. At the beginning of the 20th century as many as 21 mills were located in the valley.

From a local government point of view, in 1937 the three townships of Soyland, Rishworth and Barkisland with Ripponden united to become Ripponden Urban District Council, which enjoyed wide ranging responsibilities of administration. Prior to this each of the townships enjoyed its own system of self government. On 1st April, 1974 the Urban District Council, by an act of 1972, relinquished its power of administration and became a Parish Council.

By amalgamating with nine other local councils within the new Metropolitan Borough of Calderdale, Ripponden and its surrounding townships became part of the Metropolitan County of West Yorkshire which covers the towns of Halifax, Leeds, Bradford, Wakefield and Huddersfield. Calderdale covers an area of 138 square miles with a population of approximately 190,000. This makes it one of the smallest metropolitan districts. Approximately 20 per cent of the land is more than 1,200 ft above sea level and 27 per cent has a slope of about 1 in 10, this factor proving to be a constraint upon its industrial and residential development, particularly in the Ryburn area which is predominantly upland in character.

Much of modern Ripponden comprises a conservation area which embraces both banks of the river which are linked by a fine pack horse bridge. The conservation area contains the church, cottages, a centuries old inn and a farm museum. Textiles no longer dominate the valley having been superseded by a variety of industries which include foam plastics, car components, chemicals, plastic feed bags etc. Paper is still manufactured and Rishworth Mill, which was courageously built during the 1860s cotton slump, now produces carpet yarn. At Kebroyd Mills synthetic fibres are processed but of the cotton mills only one remains in production.

Agriculture is still practised and happily, at least from a visual point of view, new farming methods only have limited application due to the physical nature of the land. Sheep farming, cattle rearing and dairy and poultry production predominate, much of the land being used for hay making. Many acres which have been farmed have returned to the wild, often due to the construction of reservoirs rather than neglect. The nature of the land, being in the heart of the Pennines, makes it ideal for water catchment and hence the construction of reservoirs, there being six main reservoirs in the locality.

A view of the Rishworth terminus and approach road. The mill complex on the left is Commercial Mills, which is now used for industrial units.   R. Dyson Collection

A view of the railway line at Thorpe Mills which were located between the main road through the valley and the railway. Today, only some of the buildings remain which are used by a company of vehicle dismantlers.   R. Dyson Collection

Chapter Two
A Railway reaches Sowerby Bridge

The railway came to Sowerby Bridge on 5th October, 1840 with the opening of the line between Normanton and Hebden Bridge. This was the first section of the route between Manchester and Normanton, the existing connection between Leeds and Normanton leading to the Manchester and Leeds Railway, which in 1847 was to be renamed the Lancashire and Yorkshire Railway.

The journey at the time between Manchester and Leeds involved travelling by coach between Littleborough and Hebden Bridge, as the railway between these two villages still had to be completed, the work taking a further six months.

The following article appeared in the *Wakefield Journal* of 16th October, 1840 recording the opening of the railway, which gives an indication of the euphoria which existed and was still to come in the case of the Ryburn Valley:

Very Funny but Very Dangerous Doings

At the opening last week at Sowerby Bridge especially, the crowd of people was so great and the rush so alarming that, after a stay of four minutes, it was thought necessary for the train to move on. There being no room in the carriages, the adventurous travellers mounted the tops: but those who could not sit stood upright until the whole of the carriages were covered with a crowd of standers and they thus travelled to Hebden Bridge, stooping down as they passed under the tunnel and the numerous bridges on the line. We have seldom witnessed a more alarming scene. The train was proceeding at 20 m.p.h. and if a single individual had failed to stoop at the moment of passing under a bridge his brains must have been dashed out and the fall of one person must have thrown many others off the carriages to their inevitable destruction.

In the afternoon at Brighouse many passengers again mounted the roofs. Some shrewd person – we suspect Capt. Laws (Manager M & L) as the piece of strategy was worthy of the British Navy – seeing this load was too much for the carriage springs, or for the engine to draw, ordered out a waggon used for the conveyance of cattle in which those on the tops of the carriages were told they might be accommodated. Instantly the crews descended to the decks and entered the cattle waggon which was crowded to excess, and as soon as this was accomplished the train set off, leaving the waggon behind, to the infinite amusement and applause of the spectators.

In spite of the above not everyone necessarily supported the venture, as the noise and smoke spoiled a peaceful countryside and valuable agricultural land was taken up. There were objections from the Turnpike Trusts and from two canal companies, the Calder and Hebble Navigation and the Rochdale Canal Company. The following advertisement, which appeared in the *Halifax Guardian* a few weeks after the opening of the railway and refers to a reduction in fares on the stage coaches, gives further evidence that not everyone was totally in favour of the railway:

Reduction of Fares

The public are respectfully informed that the fares have been reduced by the RED ROVER and ROCKINGHAM COACHES, to BRADFORD and LEEDS.

The RED ROVER every morning at seven o'clock (except Sunday), from Carr's

Railmotor No. 8 with L&Y coach No. 13 seen here at Sowerby Bridge.

R. Brook Collection

The entrance from Slitheroe bridge to the station approach bridge showing the Lancashire and Yorkshire Railway Company sign, which reads:

L&YR.Co.
NO TRACTION ENGINE OR
ROAD ROLLER TO PASS
OVER THIS BRIDGE,
BY ORDER.

R. Dyson Collection

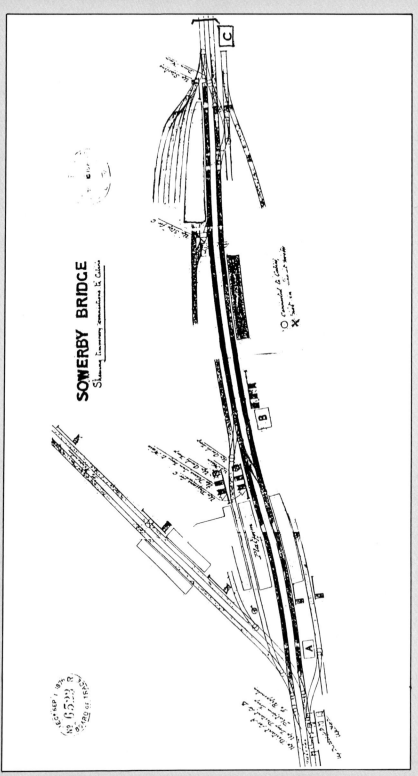

Plan of Sowerby Bridge Junction taken from the file containing documents authorising the opening of the new station (file dated 20th July 1877). It is interesting to note the platforms on the Rishworth Branch, which were never constructed in this form. The goods yard is the site of the former station and it appears that the platforms are still shown.

Courtesy P.R.O. Kew

Coach office and Northgate Hotel, Halifax, by Way of Wyke and Driglington to Leeds and returns, by the same route, from the Bull and Mouth and the Golden Lion Inns, Leeds, at five o'clock in the evening.

The ROCKINGHAM, from Carr's Coach office and the Northgate Hotel, Halifax, every morning at eight o'clock (except Sunday) by way of Bradford to Leeds, and arrives in time for the Rockingham to LONDON, at ten o'clock; returns in the afternoon at four o'clock, from the Bull and Mouth and Golden Lion, Leeds, to Bradford and Halifax.

FARES:– HALIFAX TO LEEDS
INSIDE ......5s.   OUTSIDE ...... 3s.
Performed by the public's most obedient servant,
CROSSLAND, LEE & OUTHWAITE.
Northgate Hotel, Halifax, Nov. 2 1840.

The original Sowerby Bridge Station was situated some 30 yds from the tunnel mouth. Subsequent development of the town took place in an easterly direction which led interested parties, in 1860, to consider petitioning the Lancashire and Yorkshire Railway to construct a new station. Such a station was eventually constructed on the present site which is 28 chains from the original location. The former station became part of the goods yard and the buildings were demolished.

In 1845 a possible branch line up the Ryburn Valley from a junction at Sowerby Bridge was surveyed by Richard Carter under the direction of John Hawkshaw. The scheme was to have terminated at Ripponden, and was shown leaving the main line at the east end of Sowerby Bridge tunnel by a junction facing Manchester. This latter indicates that it was considered purely as a local line and not as part of a shortened main line. The line was included in the Parliamentary plans for the West Riding Union Scheme but appears to have been left out of the Bill deposited before Parliament in 1846.

The West Riding Union Railways Company was formed following discussions between a number of smaller companies to promote several lines in the West Riding of Yorkshire. John Hawkshaw was Engineer to the company, the plans and sections for the various lines being prepared by Richard Carter. The Bill of 1846, which was to receive Royal Assent on 18th August of that year, made provision for 45½ miles of railway and included the following:

1. Sowerby Bridge to Halifax and Bradford.
2. Wyke to Brighouse.
3. Low Moor to Thornhill via Cleckheaton and Heckmondwike.
4. Heckmondwike to Mirfield.

Perhaps at this stage brief mention should be made of John Hawkshaw, who was to be a dominant figure in the development of the Lancashire and Yorkshire Railway. He was born in 1811, son of a West Riding farmer, and educated at Leeds Grammar School. Initially, after leaving school, he became involved in the construction of turnpike roads in Yorkshire. His railway interests commenced in 1829 with involvement in the survey of the Manchester and Bolton Railway, followed in 1832 by experience in Venezuela on behalf of the Bolivar Mining Association. He returned home in 1834 due to ill health and worked for a time in Liverpool and then assisted

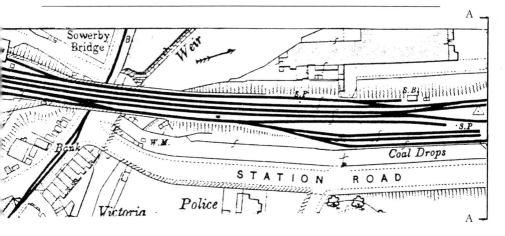

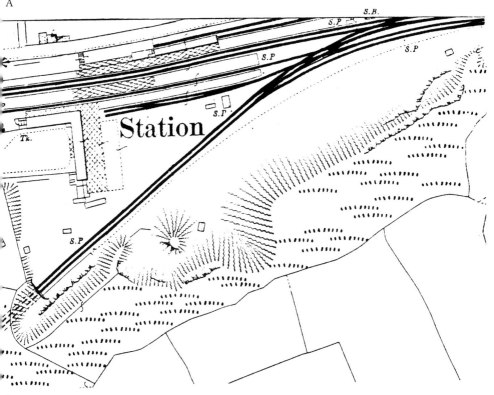

A   Sowerby Bridge station and Scar Head Tunnel. The Rishworth branch platform at
     Sowerby Bridge is not yet shown.
     Reproduced from the 1907, 25″ Ordnance Survey Map

in laying out the Leipzig and Dresden Railway. In 1836, at the age of 25, and with considerable engineering experience already gained, he was engaged to take charge of the works on the construction of the railway at Bolton.

He was subsequently appointed Chief Engineer to the Lancashire and Yorkshire Railway Company, which he retained until the end of 1850. In that year he relinquished the full time position but remained as the company's Consulting Engineer until 1888. At the same time he also served the Madras and the Eastern Bengal Railways in a similar capacity. After his retirement from the Lancashire and Yorkshire Railway he lived only another 2½ years, dying on 2nd June, 1891 at the age of 80.

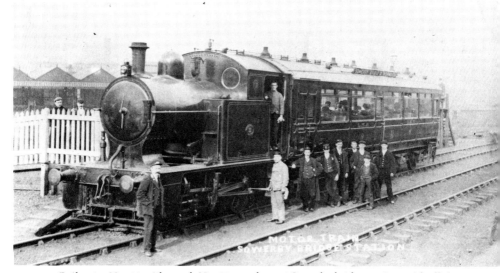

Railmotor No. 11 with coach No. 11 seen here at Sowerby bridge station, with all the staff also in attendance. The platform was built for the introduction of the railmotor service in 1907. Note the canopy over the main line platforms and also the coach nameboard which states SOWERBY BRIDGE & RISHWORTH.   *R. Brook Collection*

RIPPONDEN.

RIPPONDEN RAILWAY BAND.—Under this heading a circular has been issued, stating that "It is proposed by the inhabitants of the Ryburn district to purchase instruments and to form a band under the above designation, the performers being comprised, chiefly of the members of the late Kebroyd Mills Band, recently broken up in consequence of having been engaged in the festivities at Ripponden on the passing of the railway bill. It is proposed, therefore, to call a meeting by circular, at which a committee will be formed to transact all business in connection with the purchase of instruments and general management of the band. The instruments will remain the property of the subscribers, the performers having the free use of them, subject only to such regulations as the committee may from time to time deem requisite. Subscription lists are circulating in the district, and the liberal contributions of the inhabitants and friends are earnestly solicited. Several gentleman have promised to subscribe handsomely to the project, and it is hoped that the funds placed at the disposal of the committee will be such as to enable them to purchase first-class instruments, and to create a band that will be at once a credit and a delight to the neighbourhood."

THE HALIFAX GUARDIAN, JULY 29, 1865.

Chapter Three
The Ripponden Branch Railway Bill is passed

After a gap of 18 years the proposal to develop a railway through the Ryburn Valley was re-opened in 1864. Plans were deposited by the Lancashire and Yorkshire Railway Company for consideration in the 1865 Parliamentary session. This time the plans were prepared by Sturgess Meek, who had been appointed Resident Engineer of the Lancashire and Yorkshire Railway on 6th July, 1853, following the resignation of John Hawkshaw. He was appointed at a salary of £800 a year.

The new plan commenced at Sowerby Bridge with the junction facing Leeds. It altered the position of Ripponden Station from the 1846 proposal to a location on the west side of the river. The line was to be 2 miles 76 chains long, crossing the Ryburn on a bridge 55 ft above the river bed to a terminus near the Ripponden town centre.

In the Parliamentary proceedings it was mentioned that there were 38 mills in the Valley and they had to pay 2s. 4d. to 3s. per ton to transport coal from Sowerby Bridge. The railway was to reduce this to 2d. or 3d. per ton. Additionally domestic coal consumption was 14,600 tons per year, and it was expected to make the line very profitable to the people of the district.

1865 then was to be the year the Ryburn Valley Railway Bill was to receive Royal Assent. In spite of the obvious general desire for the construction of such a railway, however, the Bill did not have an entirely smooth passage through Parliament, and a look at the developments through the year is of interest.

The first reference in the local press, the *Halifax Guardian*, was on Saturday 4th March, 1865, when the following article appeared (the paper was only produced weekly at this time):

Ripponden – The Proposed Railway

On Wednesday evening, a meeting was held at the Queens Arms Hotel, to discuss the proposed railway. Messrs Horsfall and Wardle, of Halifax, the surveyors of the line attended. The feeling was evidently in favour of the railway, and many influential inhabitants were present.

The following Saturday, 11th March, 1865, reference was again made to the meeting, and the first signs of dissension hinted at:

Ripponden – The Railway Movement

In last Saturday's *Guardian* it was stated that a meeting of the millowners and owners of property in the neighbourhood was held at the Queens Arms, on the evening of Shrove Tuesday. It was decided to draw up a petition to the Houses of Parliament in favour of the Ripponden branch from Sowerby Bridge, which we are glad to say has been very numerously signed, being headed by the members of the three local boards, Soyland, Rishworth and Barkisland. The day appointed for the decision in this matter is Monday, March 13th. Photographers have been busy this week taking several views on the line of the route proposed to be taken by the branch railway. Both the opposition and the Lancashire and Yorkshire have had their men employed, and much amusement was caused by one of them trying a whole day to gain a view of the valley and yet not have a house or chimney visible in it. It is supposed that he scarcely succeeded.

On Monday 3rd April, 1865 the proposal to build a branch line between Sowerby Bridge and Ripponden was heard by a court of referees in the

21

A fine close-up view of railmotor No. 9 at Rishworth station. Note the paintwork scheme on the platform canopy valance.   *R. Dyson Collection*

A general view of Rishworth station from across the other side of the valley. The approach bridge can be seen in the centre of the picture and also note the extensive goods traffic around the station.   *R. Dyson Collection*

House of Commons. The court was chaired by Michael D. Hassard and included Sir W. Gibson Craig and Colonel Stewart.

The petitioners against the Bill were Messrs W.H. and F.E. Rawson, and Mr R. Ridehalgh. Only Messrs Rawson appeared before the referees. Also in attendance were the Engineers, Hawkshaw and Meek, and the Surveyors, Horsfall and Mallinson.

The major concern was expressed in engineering terms about the junction with the main line at Sowerby Bridge, although comment was made about the route through the valley, even to the point of suggesting a route up the other side be looked at.

On consideration of all the evidence given the referees expressed the opinion "that there are no engineering objections to the junctions as proposed and that they may be safely made". They also expressed the opinion that the line could not well be carried in any other way up the valley than that proposed, but they considered that a screen should be erected and kept up by the railway company (if requested to do so) between the turnpike road and the railway.

Although the following report appeared in the *Halifax Guardian* on 8th April, 1865 conveying the local feelings about the referees' decision, a report of the formal confirmation of the decision did not appear until 6th May, 1865 when it stated that the referees had reported to the House of Commons.

Ripponden – The Railway

The arrival of a telegram from London in the village on Monday evening announcing the passing of the Ripponden Branch Railway Bill by the referees in the House of Commons was productive of no small amount of excitement and satisfaction. A number of gentlemen had assembled in anticipation of the message, and the news was hailed with great enthusiasm. On Tuesday evening a meeting of manufacturers and landowners was held at the Queens Arms Inn, when the peculiar character of the opposition offered by the Messrs Rawson and Mr Ridehalgh, who are the only opposing petitioners, was discussed. These gentlemen claim to be heard against the Bill on engineering details, cost of construction, and efficiency of the works. The liberal conduct of other landowners, who not only showed no feeling against the inhabitants of the district participating in the advantages of railway accommodation, but were willing to aid in any possible manner the aquisition of so great a boon, was also alluded to. The meeting unanimously pledged itself to support the scheme with the utmost vigour, and to further in every possible way the endeavours of the Lancashire and Yorkshire Railway Company to obtain the powers sought in the Bill now before Parliament. On Thursday there was another meeting held, and Mr R. Horsfall, the Surveyor of the proposed line, was present by invitation. A conversation ensued, but was principally confined to technical details. Allusion was made to the clause in the Bill wherein the restrictive period of five years is named for the completion of the line, and although the meeting was assured by Mr Horsfall that the company would proceed with the execution of the works immediately upon the Bill receiving the Royal Assent, it was resolved unanimously that the directors be memorialised to shorten the restricted time of completion to four years. A requisition to this effect will therefore be submitted to the manufacturers and others for signature in due course.

It was to be another 13 years before Ripponden obtained its railway but there was obviously a keen sense of optimism that it could be constructed much quicker. This optimism can be seen throughout the period of incep-

A railmotor at Triangle station about 1909. The 'up' line is the only one in use. The coaches on the right are being stored and were largely used for excursion and special traffic.   *R. Dyson Collection*

Triangle station situated on sharp curves (note check rails) looking towards Sowerby Bridge. The station consisted solely of two wooden-framed platforms filled with ash.
R. Dyson Collection

tion and construction and the numerous setbacks which affected the scheme in no way appeared to dampen the enthusiasm of all concerned.

Following the report of the referees an enquiry was held before a committee in the House of Commons. This commenced on Tuesday 16th May, 1865, the committee consisting of Mr J.H. Rogers (Chairman), Mr Benyon, Mr Blake and Mr Morgan. The Lancashire and Yorkshire Railway Bill under consideration had six objects, one of which was "to make the following railway, length two miles and seventy-six chains from a junction with their main line at Sowerby Bridge to Lower Brig Royd at Ripponden."

The Bill was opposed by Mr R. Ridehalgh, Messrs Rawson and Messrs Tweedale. Mr Hope Scott, Mr Merryweather, Mr Vernon Harcourt and Mr Hope were engaged for the promotors of the Bill; Mr West and Mr Western Price for the opponents. The majority of the Bill was unopposed. The main opposition was to the Ripponden line, the opponents being mill owners.

The following interesting facts were brought out: "In the valley of Ripponden there were 38 mills, using 6,800 tons of raw material, sending out 9,000 tons of manufactured goods, and using 33,000 tons of coal, making altogether a total of 50,000 tons, all of which was now conveyed in carts."

The Messrs Rawson objected that their land would be intersected by the railway, and Mr W.H. Rawson further complained that his residence, Mill House at Sowerby Bridge, would be cut up and seriously injured, whilst the railway would not assist in the carriage of their goods. Mr W.H. Rawson had a mill and dye-works on one side of the river and the railway was to be on the other. He had recently purchased property in the Valley between Mill House and Sowerby Bridge, at a cost of £16,000, which would be disected by the railway.

Mr F. Rawson resided at Thorpe House and worked a mill 125 yards from the railway. His objection was injury to his property and being deprived of the use of a stream or goit for his mill. It was determined, however, that his use of the stream would not be affected.

Mr Ridehalgh resided at the Ripponden end of the line and complained that the line would injuriously affect his property at Brig Royd, by destroying trees, cutting up ornamental land, destroying access to the road, and overlooking the gardens and grounds.

The case against the Ripponden line was not heard until the second day of the enquiry, Wednesday 17th May, 1865. It was noted that "the Ripponden line is heavy, speaking generally, but for Yorkshire the works are light". Mr Ridehalgh, the first petitioner, was a solicitor. Only the station would be visible from his house at Brig Royd.

In regard to Mr F. Rawson of Thorpe House, it was noted that all the mill premises lay between the line and the house. At Mill House, which is nearer Sowerby Bridge, home of Mr W.H. Rawson, the mill and the river came between the house and the line. Both were woollen mills.

Under examination Mr Hawkshaw pointed out that it was virtually the same line as was surveyed in 1846, although the termini were different. It was noted that at Ripponden there were four mills close to the station with six more a little further on. It was pointed out that there would be no difficulty in providing sidings for the mills at Thorpe House and Mill House if they were wanted.

A fine study of locomotive No. 218, 0–6–2T seen here at Triangle station. The service was travelling from Rishworth to Sowerby Bridge and was photographed around 1900 when both platforms were in use.

R. Dyson Collection

Mr Richard Horsfall, actual surveyor of the line, informed the Committee that within the last twelve years he had erected mills in the Ripponden Valley, including 5 or 6 entirely new, with engines and machinery, to the value of £100,000. The mills were for wool, cotton and silk. He further pointed out that if the Bill were passed he would immediately let a large mill at Barkisland. He expressed surprise at Mr Ridehalgh's opposition as the station building would be superior to the building he looked out onto at this time. He also expressed the view that woollen mills such as those belonging to the Rawsons caused more nuisance from noise, smoke, steam and smells than anything likely to arise from a railway.

At this stage it appeared the general desire was for a line to Ripponden and there was no proposal to extend to Rishworth.

Major Stansfield, who owned considerable property in the neighbourhood of the line was cross-examined and expressed his total support for the project.

Mr J.W. Cartwright, managing partner of Messrs Wheelwright at Dyson Lane and Small Lees Mills, and also owner of 400 acres of land, was cross-examined. He pointed out their mills employed 500 hands, their new mills would employ 200 more. They consumed 638 tons of wool a year being carted from Sowerby Bridge at 3s. 4d. a ton average. The proposed line would give a saving of 2s. – 3s. a ton. They consumed 3,000 tons of coal a year, again the line would save 2s. – 3s. cartage. They consumed 536 tons of cotton a year, then sent by cart from Manchester. The railway would save 6s. or 7s. a ton on the raw material and 3s. or 4s. a ton on the manufactured goods sent out. He had recently built a mill at Rishworth and considered that the area was growing in importance and required a railway. He expected coal consumption to go up to 4,000 to 5,000 tons a year. He had four brothers, all mill owners employing 600 to 700 hands, all in favour of the line.

Mr John Bradley, a Rishworth farmer, made the case for the railway for the carting of local stone, wood and of importing lime. He apparently stated, amongst laughter, that he believed he faced in that room all the opponents of the railway (namely Messrs Rawson and Mr Ridehalgh). The quarries were in the Valley above Ripponden.

Mr Mellor, a farmer and papermaker from Ripponden, explained that he got nearly all his paper materials from Sowerby Bridge by cart. Lime, allum, coals, general goods etc. all were carted from Sowerby Bridge at 3s. 6d. a ton. This would be saved by the formation of the railway and he had never heard any of his neighbours speak against the line.

Other speakers in favour of the line included Mr Gilpan, managing partner of Holt and Company, cotton manufacturers at Slitheroe Mills; Mr J. Cocker, director of a new joint stock mill company (limited) at Ripponden; Mr Joseph Sutcliffe, clerk to the board at Soyland.

Mr James Smithies, traffic manager of the Lancashire and Yorkshire Railway, revealed a few interesting facts. In the previous year the company carried 18 million passengers at an average of 10 miles each, each paying an average of 9.3 pence. As opportunities presented themselves branch lines were constructed into the valleys. The proposed line would run up to within a short distance of the last mill. All the mills in the Ryburn Valley would be

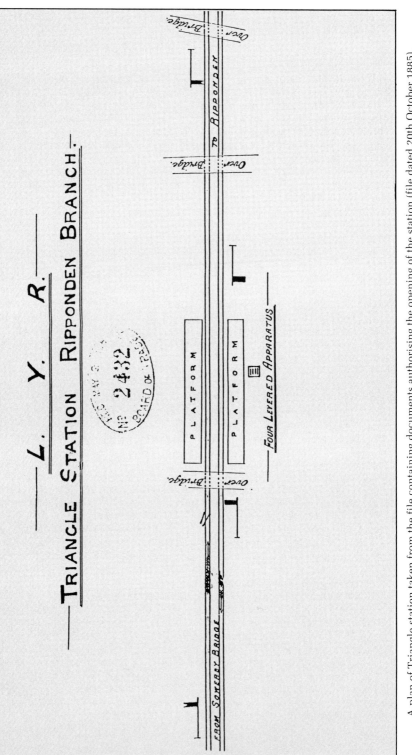

A plan of Triangle station taken from the file containing documents authorising the opening of the station (file dated 20th October 1885).
Courtesy P.R.O., Kew, Ref. MT6/396/13

within free delivery distance. It would be like removing Sowerby Bridge station to Ripponden. The coal would pay 3*d*. a ton more at Ripponden than at Sowerby Bridge. On further examination he stated that, in his opinion, a tunnel through the backbone of England in order to carry the line towards Rochdale, would be a useless expenditure of money.

Witnesses were then called in support of the opposition: Mr G. Hadwin of Kebroyd Mill, a silk mill, also a trustee of the turnpike road (he pointed out that the desire had always been for a through communication with Lancashire); Mr Morris of the Lodge, Triangle, owner and occupier of Stansfield Mill (he thought the line would be so high that he could not obtain a siding).

Having heard the evidence the Committee came down in favour of the line, the following report, which is worth quoting in full, appearing in the *Halifax Guardian* of 27th May, 1865:

THE RAILWAY – The recent enquiry held before a Committee in the House of Commons respecting the merits of the scheme for making a branch railway from Sowerby Bridge to Ripponden has been watched with the keenest interest by the whole population of the district. We have already given a report of the proceedings in Parliament from Tuesday to Friday in last week, when the hearing was adjourned until Monday; and on that day the Committee, after consulting about seven minutes, gave their decision in favour of the Bill. During the investigation of the case every scrap of news from the "Big Town" was greedily sought after at Ripponden; and every evening the village was dotted by groups of men discussing the topic of the day "to be or not to be". On Saturday evening last some of the gentlemen who had been up in London on behalf of the promoters, returned, and were received with considerable demonstrations, and besieged with queries relative to the issue of the enquiry. As on Monday, the decision was expected, the excitement became intense and as the afternoon wore on the inhabitants congregated in the open part of the village, anxiously awaiting the arrival of the all-important telegram. At a few minutes to five o'clock a man arrived in breathless haste, having out-run the messenger and communicated the welcome intelligence that the "Ripponden Branch Line Bill" was passed, and in a few minutes after a telegram was received from the House of Commons, confirming the news. The report spread like wildfire and probably before an hour had elapsed every cottage in the district was startled with the cry of "HOORA, THEYN GETTEN T'RAILWAI". From the roar and rattle of the artillery, consisting of two small cannon, divers and various single and double guns, pistols, and revolvers – the merry peal of the village bells, the hoisting of banners etc., a stranger sojourning in the place would certainly conclude that the ancestral bogies, the French, had of a verity suddenly landed at either Dover Castle or at Spring Rock, on Norland Moor! Not to be unheard in the general gunnery, the students of the college quickly unlimbered their old favourite piece d'ordnance "Little Bull Dog", and soon his vociferous bark was heard amongst the hills, contributing to the "harmony" of the evening. About six o'clock, nearly all the manufacturers of the neighbourhood had come down to the village, and a band of music arriving opportunely at the same moment, it was at once determined to engage it and form a procession to Triangle.

The worthy Mayor was consulted, and he immediately accepted the post of honour in the van, after being duly decorated with the mayoral chain and attended by the mace bearer in his scarlet uniform. Marshalled by two impromptu adjutants, the procession was speedily *en route*, amid deafening cheers, the discharge of firearms, the shooting of the bells, and the clash and clang of the band. The dwellers in high places along the valley gravitated to the turnpike road, and on the

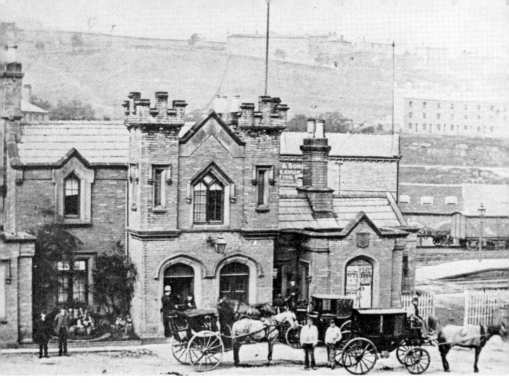

Sowerby Bridge Old Station. Opened in 1840, this station was replaced on 1st September, 1876 by the present station located at the junction with the Rishworth line. *Courtesy Calderdale Libraries*

A view of Ripponden and Barkisland station looking towards Rishworth with a rail-motor in attendance. *R. Brook Collection*

cavalcade entering the celebrated equilateral of the village of Triangle, the procession extended a distance of half a mile, four deep, and in very tolerable order. Arriving at the baths, the procession counter-marched and returned to Ripponden in good form and as hilarious as ever about eleven o'clock. Under the prompt and energetic action of adjutants Y and Z this peripatetic demonstration was a decided success. The cavalcade returned by the Old Bridge and the Golden Lion, and was dispersed at the Queens Arms Inn; refreshments *ad libertum* having been distributed on the line of the march. Nothing now remained to complete the tableau but the presence of the three expected witnesses, on their way from London. The scene was now an exceedingly animated one.

The carriage containing the three gentlemen, who had remained in London to hear the finale, and who now brought the "full and true particulars of the decision of the Parliamentary committee", and "the last dying speech of the opposition". The arrival was the signal of such an outburst of popular feeling as never before awoke the echoes of Ripponden hills.

In spite of all this euphoria consent had still not been obtained to construct the line as it still had to be authorised by the House of Lords. On Monday 26th June, 1865 the Bill came up for consideration before the Lords Committee, which consisted of The Duke of Montrose (Chairman), The Earl of Albermarle, The Earl of Verulan, Lord Harris and Lord Seymour.

It was noted that the Lancashire and Yorkshire Railway was initiated as long ago as 1845, but that in 1847, the year of the panic, many schemes fell through. The Ripponden branch was one of those thrown out by the panic. It was further stated that there was some opposition to the present Bill on the part of the landowners. It was not considered formidable as it was overcome in the Commons, but nevertheless it necessitated some explanation of the line:

> Its length was two miles, seven furlongs and six chains. It commenced by a junction with the Lancashire and Yorkshire line at Sowerby Bridge, running through a tunnel at Scout Head entered into the Ripponden Valley, went to Mill House, the property of Mr W.H. Rawson, then to Thorpe Mill, the property of his brother, Mr Frederick Rawson, passed along the hillside into a cutting, and ultimately reached the manufacturing village of Ripponden, at a place of convenient access to the mills, and where, if an extension of the line should be demanded, the extension could be made under favourable circumstances.

> The company were in connection with the Barnsley coalfields, and it would be a vast advantage to the Ripponden people to have their coals carried to them by railway, instead of being carted, as they were at present, from Sowerby Bridge. And so with regard to their receipt of raw material, and sending away of manufactured article.

The cost of the line was estimated at £75,000.

The road trustees had now added their opposition to the Bill. Certain other landowners, Messrs Hadwin Kirkman, Priestley and John Field Wright, also added their opposition. The line at this stage was to be a single line with land and bridges for a double line. It was noted that the owner of cottages on the proposed site of Ripponden Station, a Mr Jennings, was a petitioner in favour of the line.

Upon completion of the enquiry the House of Lords declared itself in favour of the line, this being duly reported in the *Halifax Guardian* on 1st July, 1865:

> RIPPONDEN THE RAILWAY – The excitement, consequent upon the passing of the Ripponden Branch Railway Bill in the House of Commons, had just ebbed to the ordinary quietude of village life, when the inhabitants of this enterprising district were roused once more by the fact that the Committee in the House of Lords would sit on Monday. We understand that petitions in favour of the Bill were presented to the Lords a short time ago, signed, in two days, by 1,400 residents, together with similar petitions from the local boards interested in the prosperity of the Ryburn Valley. The departure to town of the local witnesses last Saturday, contributed to increase the interest existing here as to the success of the measure. As will be seen from our report of the enquiry, the hearing extended over three days.
>
> On Wednesday the joyful news reached Ripponden that "My Lords had passed the Bill". The expression of feeling which this intelligence evoked is easier to imagine than be described. Towards evening the village became more and more crowded, innumerable visits of persons were evidently "laying down the law", or cracking jokes most hilariously. As a matter of course, the determined nature of the opposition that has been offered to the Bill has very considerably tended to create an interest and a degree of feeling that would not otherwise have existed. The return of the witnesses was expected at Halifax by the 9.12 train, and a coach with four greys was engaged to convey them on to Ripponden. The party arrived at "Ryburn's capital" at about 10 o'clock and were received with all the traditional hurrahs and noise and pomp, and circumstances of triumphal entries! "The Mayor" presided at "a convivial" held in the large room at the Queen Hotel and the company present celebrated the occasion in the usual manner, and with the greatest enthusiasm – *Nota Bene* – A correspondent writes to inform us that the 27 guns which were fired in St James' Park immediately the decision was given by the Chairman of the Committee, was not, as he supposed, the celebration of such verdict, but had something he believed in connection with the Queen's Coronation!!!

Royal assent was finally given to the Bill on 5th July, 1865 and so, at last, the stage was set for the construction of a railway up the Ryburn Valley as far as Ripponden. As mentioned earlier the estimated cost of building the line was £75,000 with a five year construction period. Capital of £140,000 was authorised by the Bill plus a further £46,000 by loan, although this sum was to include the construction of the nearby Stainland branch.

At this time the Lancashire and Yorkshire Railway Company was heavily committed on other schemes and consequently was unlikely to proceed rapidly with the Ripponden branch which was not expected to show a large return on the capital outlay. Unfortunately both the cost and construction period estimates were to prove highly optimistic and to be far exceeded, but that will come later.

Chapter Four
Eight Years of Little Progress

It was not until 1873 that construction of the railway was to commence. It must have been a disappointment after the euphoria of 1865 that eight years were to elapse before any visual evidence of progress was to be seen. Nevertheless these intervening years were not entirely lacking in action and a brief resumé of the significant events is of interest before looking in some detail at the year in question.

The initial Act of 1865 envisaged a construction period of five years, but by 1868 it had become obvious that it was unlikely that even a start would have been made within this period. So consequently, on 25th June, 1868, an Act was passed extending the construction period to 5th July, 1872. Subsequent events, however, were to prove even this insufficient. The acquisition of land for the railway was slowly progressing at this time.

In 1869 a further extension of the construction period was authorised, this being to 11th June, 1873. It was also in this year that plans were prepared for an extension to Rishworth, this being considered a first stage in the construction of a line to Littleborough which was seen as an alternative shorter version to the existing main line through Hebden Bridge and Todmorden. The extension to Rishworth was to be one mile seventy-four chains in length diverging from the authorised line and climbing up the east bank of the river.

The approval of the extension to Rishworth came in 1870. The Lancashire and Yorkshire Railway Act of that year allowed the company to abandon almost one mile of the line authorised in 1865, this being the section which would have crossed the River Ryburn. The change meant that the objection to the original proposal by Mr Ridehalgh had belatedly been upheld.

The abandoned section was substituted by an authority to construct an extension one mile seventy-four chains in length, to a site fourteen chains beyond the eventual Rishworth (Slitheroe) terminus which was constructed. The additional length would have involved constructing a bridge over the Ripponden–Oldham road. Deviation from the original line was one mile seventy-nine and a half chains from Sowerby Bridge. The bridge over the Elland Road, alongside Ripponden Station, was of 35 ft span and 16 ft above road level. The proposed terminus would have been alongside Rishworth School and, in addition to the road bridge, would have included a "viaduct" over the River Ryburn 180 yds long, and with a height of 78 ft above the river bed. The terminal station was planned as "Slitheroe" but was always known as Rishworth.

In the same year, 1870, the time for the purchase of land was extended to 5th July, 1871, and for the completion of the entire branch to 5th July, 1874.

And so to 1873, when, on 10th May, tenders were invited for the construction of the railway. On 11th June the contract for the line was let to a Mr James Evans for £95,404. Following enquiries by Sturges Meek, however, this was rescinded. No details appear to be available in support of this decision, the only recorded comment being that Mr Evans proved himself to be unsuitable.

On 18th June, 1873 the contract was offered to Mr T.J. Waller for the sum of £113,000. This price was considered high, some 20 per cent higher than

This view, taken before 1907, shows the railway line at Watson's Mills before the construction of the halt.

R. Dyson Collection

Mr Evans' figure, but the contractor refused to reduce it and Sturges Meek appears to have been supportive of him. Mr Waller's tender was finally accepted on 25th June, 1873, and on the same date a tender was accepted for the construction of the new Sowerby Bridge Station which is referred to earlier in this book. The price for this job was £25,634, the firm being Dransfield, Thomson & Hulme.

Soon afterwards, on 8th July, 1873, a Resident Engineer was appointed for the Ripponden Line, this being Mr Herbert Radcliffe who was appointed at a salary of £250 per year. So the scene was set for the work to commence, and it did at last on 30th September, 1873. Once again it appears that the imagination of the local population was captured, this being embodied in the following article taken from the *Halifax Guardian* of 11th October, 1873. The article also gives an interesting description of the line itself.

THE RAILWAY: Ripponden folks are taking a lively interest in the construction of the line which is to place the village in connection with the great railway system of the country; whilst many stalwart young men with a view no doubt to being able to say when they grow old that they had a share in the work, will handle a mattock, spade or wheelbarrow, and work away heartily at the voluntary and gratuitous service for a few minutes at a time. The site for the Ripponden station is in a field behind the National School; and a beer house keeper whose place of business is amongst the jumble of houses at the bottom of Ripponden Old Bank, has taken time by the forelock, and already named his house "The Lancashire and Yorkshire Railway Hotel". Near to the site of the proposed station a considerable amount of excavation has already been done. The line towards Slitheroe will cross the new Ripponden Bank on a bridge; but in the other direction it will be conducted under the Old Bank, and for the purpose it has been found necessary to slightly deviate from the original plan. After emerging from the bridge at this point it will proceed in a short cutting behind the house of Mr Greenwood and then crossing Hanging Stones Lane, will be conducted in front of the farm of that name (appropriately so called as it is situated under a mass of overhanging rocks) on an embankment across a ravine and fence along the fields parallel with the lane for a considerable distance, and at a great elevation above the Rhyburn. At the point where the river bends into the hill, the line has to cross the face of a precipitous piece of ground where immense retaining walls will have to be erected. Considerable excavations have been made at this point and the level of the line made for several hundreds of yards, no doubt with the intention of getting in as soon as possible of a single line of rails so that stone and other material may be brought for the heavy retaining walls and other works necessary here and at a point lower down where the line will pass along the face of another precipice near the waterfall. Hanging Stones Lane is again crossed and cut-up for about one hundred yards so that it will require diverting either under or over the line which proceeds forward by another cutting along the fields belonging to Little Haven Farm and enters Rough Hey Wood at the point where it is now entered by the footpath, leading from the stepping stones near Denton Bridge to Stansfield Mill. In Rough Hey Wood the timber has been cleared and the works will not be of a heavy character. The line at this point will be almost entirely concealed from view of passers on the turnpike road, and will be out of sight from Thorpe, the residence of Mr F.E. Rawson, passing under Rough Hey, across the land now in the occupation of Mr H. Norris, the line will run across the two roads now leading from Stansfield Mill to Norland, and in the vicinity of which will be the station for Triangle; and beyond this will proceed along the Norland side of the valley, past Mill House, and so forward, by a gentle descent to its junction with the main line at the end of Mereclough cutting. At the upper part, most of the works will be of a comparatively light character; but between Triangle and Sowerby Bridge, the material to cut through will be harder and the works slower, as in this direction there will the principal cuttings and tunnelling. The works have been commenced with considerable energy and navvies are engaged at six different points. At Sowerby Bridge end, lines of rails have been laid, and the use of the wheelbarrow for tipping has been superseded by the well-known contractor's railway waggons. As the line is to be completed within a year it will need all this energy and we hope that before the end of 1874, Ripponden people may see their wishes accomplished.

Unfortunately the prediction at the end of this article was to prove far too optimistic as it was to be another five years before the railway was completed, and this only as far as Ripponden.

A view of the Ryburn Valley with Rishworth station seen in the background just above the mill.   R. Dyson Collection

Chapter Five
Construction and Opening

And so the year finally arrived when the Ryburn Valley was to see trains. The fact that the construction period for the section to Ripponden was five years, and it was to be another three years before the extension to Rishworth opened for traffic, indicated that many problems had been met. Before getting to the actual events of 1878, it is interesting to look briefly at the events in the intervening years after construction commenced in 1873.

On 11th March, 1874 the contract for the construction of iron bridges along the line was let to a firm called Rankin for the sum of £3165. The date for the completion of the whole line was extended to 5th July, 1874. A further extension due to the troubles which were being experienced was approved by Parliament on 16th July, 1874, this time the extension being to 5th July, 1876.

Problems experienced with the construction were recorded from time to time. The *Halifax Courier* of 21st May, 1875 reported that on the previous day 60 tons of shale had collapsed, killing one man in the process and several others having narrow escapes. This occurred in the cutting at Dodge Royd Wood although there had been previous landslips at Rough Hey Wood. It was necessary to lower the deep slopes in the cutting below Triangle to ensure stability.

In August of 1875 a severe landslip occurred in Rough Hey Wood leading to the proposal of a diversion involving a tunnel. Such diversion was not to materialise however. On 4th September, 1875 a report was produced relating to the construction of Scar Head tunnel and indicating that it may have to be abandoned. At that time only 200 yds of the 593 yds long tunnel had been completed at a cost of between £25,000 and £30,000. The remainder was showing signs of collapse and large quantities of timber were having to be used for support. Eventually it proved necessary to construct banks of retaining walls below rail level to prevent any slipping. The tunnel had an arch of six courses of stone work with an invert of four courses, both the tunnel portals being constructed in a castellated style.

The proposed diversion and tunnel at Rough Hey Wood was included in a Bill for the 1876 Parliamentary session but was withdrawn on 12th April, 1876 following which work went ahead to remove the land slip. A further time extension was authorised on 24th July, 1876.

On 1st September, 1876 the new station at Sowerby Bridge was opened, being located at the junction with the branch to Ripponden. The inspecting officer appointed by the Board of Trade was Major General Hutchinson, who found everything in satisfactory order. Shortly after this date the old station was demolished and a goods shed was constructed on the site. Although built at the junction with the branch, it was to be necessary for trains from Ripponden to reverse into and out of the station to gain access to the branch. An early plan of Sowerby Bridge Junction did show that double platforms were proposed for construction on the Ripponden branch, but these never materialised.

By 27th September, 1876 total expenditure had reached £199,850, this being some £86,699 in excess of the contract price. On 29th November, 1876

A fine view of Ripponden and Barkisland station from the Elland Road (note Ripponden church in the left foreground). Barkisland is on the other side of the railway.

R. Dyson Collection

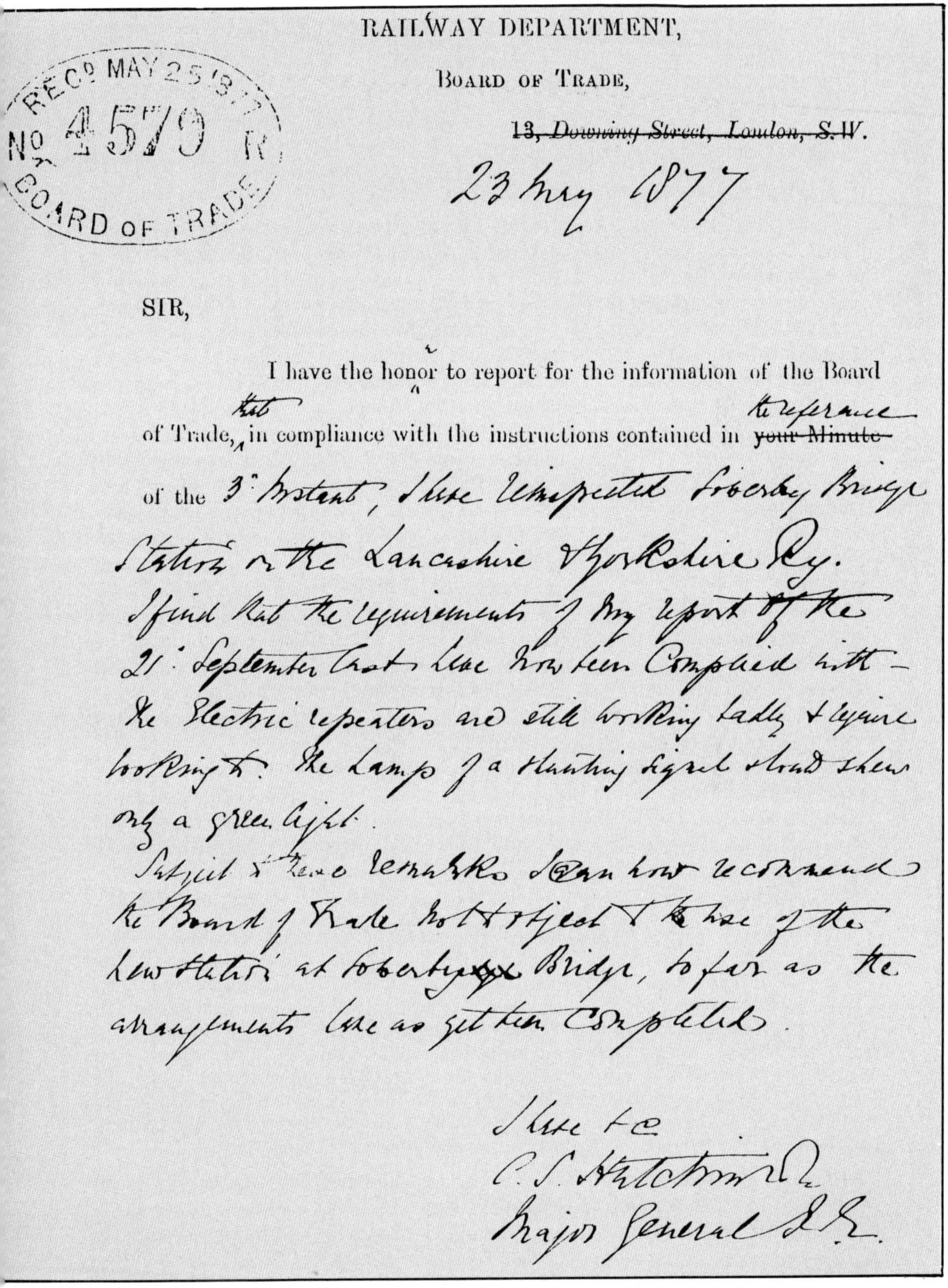

RAILWAY DEPARTMENT,

BOARD OF TRADE,

~~13, Downing Street, London, S.W.~~

23 May 1877

RECD MAY 25 '77
No 4579 R
BOARD OF TRADE

SIR,

I have the honour to report for the information of the Board of Trade, that in compliance with the instructions contained in the reference ~~your Minute~~ of the 3rd Instant, I have re-inspected Sowerby Bridge Station on the Lancashire & Yorkshire Ry.

I find that the requirements of my report ~~of the~~ 21st September last have now been complied with — the Electric repeaters are still working badly & require looking to. The Lamps of a shunting signal should shew only a green light.

Subject to these remarks I can now recommend the Board of Trade not to object to the use of the new station at Sowerby Bridge, so far as the arrangements have as yet been completed.

I have &c.
C. S. Hutchinson
Major General R.E.

A letter from the Board of Trade advising that the new station at Sowerby Bridge can be used (23rd May, 1877). *Courtesy P.R.O., Kew; Ref. MT6/184*

the following list of difficulties and attendant costs was reported:

Lower cutting and embankment slopes: £41,900
Longer wing walls as a result of the above: £2700
Retaining walls: £42,200
Increased tunnel masonry: £13,000
Additional culverts: £4200

"Ordinary contingencies" and excess in cuttings, river walls and tunnel: £62,590.

These difficulties were not considered unreasonable by the Board of Trade, however, as no further extension of time to completion was given as a result of them. At the end of 1876 the hope was expressed that, given good weather and no further accidents, the line would be completed by 1st May, 1877. Unfortunately a number of opening date predictions were still to be given and it was to be more than twelve months after this latter date before the actual opening was to take place. On 14th February, 1877 it was reported that if no further disaster took place the line should be completed by June of that year.

And so to 1878. The 16th February saw the *Halifax Guardian* reporting that "The Lancashire and Yorkshire Railway Company, in their report just issued, state that the Ripponden Branch Line is now nearly ready for inspection by the Government officer, previous to it being opened for passenger traffic. A sum of £23,500 is put down to be expended on it during the present half year". Then on 23rd March, "RIPPONDEN: THE RAILWAY STATION – both at the passenger and goods stations the works are being very energetically pushed on, those engaged having their instructions that all must be completed by the end of the month". Another less than prophetic statement appeared on 15th June, 1878 "It is stated that there is every prospect that this branch line will be opened on 1st July next, both for goods and passenger traffic".

It was apparent, however, that the line to Ripponden was almost complete and on 5th February, 1878 the Lancashire and Yorkshire Railway Company wrote to the Board of Trade indicating their intention to open the railway for public traffic. The Board of Trade appointed Major F. Marindin as the inspecting officer and the official inspection took place on 8th July, 1878. The inspection was recorded by the Halifax Guardian of 13th July, 1878:

RIPPONDEN: THE NEW RAILWAY – some excitement took place on Monday last, when it became known that the inspector had intimated to the Directory of the Lancashire and Yorkshire Railway Company that he intended making his official inspection of the line of rail recently constructed between Sowerby Bridge and Ripponden. He was met by several of the Directors, with the principal officers of the company, the party being conveyed from the Sowerby Bridge station in a saloon carriage. At the various bridges and other places, he closely examined the work, and expressed himself favourably as to the well executed and substantial character of the work. At the Slitheroe terminus the inspector and his party lunched and then proceeded on the return journey to Sowerby Bridge.

Although it appears from the above account that the inspector's train travelled to the Slitheroe (Rishworth) terminus, it was to be another three years before the section between Ripponden and Rishworth was officially

opened to traffic. Following the inspection Major Marindin issued a telegram deferring the opening of the line to passenger traffic by one month. The
reason for this was detailed in the Major's report dated the same day, which
listed the following works requiring attention:

1. Gradient boards and mile posts required.
2. Certain areas of fencing to be made good.
3. Runaway points to be installed at Ripponden.
4. Connecting rod to points at Ripponden requiring attention.
5. Clocks to be fitted at the Ripponden signal cabin and Ripponden
   station.
6. Tunnel recesses to be constructed.
7. Improvements required to the signalling at Sowerby Bridge Junction.

On 15th July, 1878 the line was officially opened for goods traffic only.
The *Halifax Guardian* of 27th July, 1878 noted that "The first truck of cattle
and sheep from Wakefield to Ripponden railway station was booked by Mr
John Whitley, butcher, White Hart Inn, Dyson Lane, on the 16th inst."

29th July, 1878 saw a further inspection when the inspecting officer
indicated that he would not object to the opening of the line on the 1st
August, 1878 subject to a notification being previously given by the Lancashire and Yorkshire Railway Company to the Board of Trade that all the
requirements contained in the report had been complied with. The report
indicated that all the points listed on the 8th July had been dealt with
other than the station clock and the connecting rod to points at Ripponden.
The only other matter mentioned was adjustment to the facing points at
Sowerby Bridge. The Lancashire and Yorkshire Railway Company con-
firmed, in a letter dated 2nd August, 1878, that the requirements in the
report will be dealt with.

And so the company was finally able to announce the date of the official
opening of the railway to passengers, this being 5th August, 1878. It was to
prove a day of great rejoicing which is again perhaps best described in the
words of the day by quoting the newspaper report which appeared in the
Halifax Guardian of 10th August, 1878:

OPENING OF THE RIPPONDEN BRANCH RAILWAY

In 1865 the sanction of Parliament was obtained for the construction of a railway
from Sowerby Bridge to Ripponden. Thirteen years afterwards viz, on Monday, 5th
August 1878, passengers were conveyed, for the first time, by train from Sowerby
Bridge to Ripponden, and from Ripponden to Sowerby Bridge, the fare charged for
a third class passenger being the low sum of 3d. There had been various causes for
the delay; but not withstanding the fact that a scheme has been before the public so
long, the inhabitants of the valley of the Ryburn celebrated the opening of the line
on Monday last with becoming enthusiasm, and there is not much doubt that if a
little more notice had been given of the opening visitors from Halifax and other
places would have patronised the new undertaking in larger numbers.

Shortly before 8.30 in the morning, a train consisting of one "composite", two
third class carriages, engine and tender, and the guard's van draws up alongside
the platform at Sowerby Bridge Station. Punctually at 8.30 am the signal was
given, the engine backed out of the station to get on the branch line and the journey
was commenced to Ripponden amid a discharge of detonating signals. The train
entered the tunnel under Scar Head, having a freight of 35 passengers, in addition
to various railway officials, amongst whom may be numbered Mr Crawshaw, the

block inspector: Mr Dews, agent, goods department; Mr Pearson, clerk in charge at
Sowerby Bridge Station; Mr Dixon, locomotive superintendent, Sowerby Bridge
(who rode on the engine); Mr W. Wilson, the guard; Mr Richard Grundy, the driver,
and Mr J. Longbottom, the stoker. The train ran very "sweetly" indeed and the
station at Ripponden was reached in seven minutes, the distance being just over
three miles, over a gently rising gradient. The arrival, amid explosions of fog
signals, booming of cannons, ringing of church bells etc., was witnessed by crowds
of people, young and old, who had crowded a bridge over the line near the station
or had taken possession of the platform.

The village itself not only wore a holiday appearance, but was gay with the
display of flags, banners, etc., in all directions. Three flags were fixed on the roof of
the station, the church steeple just beneath was decorated in a similar manner, and
at Chapel Field Mill, the commercial cotton company's factory, Dyson Lane Mill,
Rishworth Mills, and on the premises of Messrs Nathan Whitley & Son, emblems
of a similar character were displayed. The Waterloo, or Old Bridge Inn, the Golden
Lion, the Rose and Crown, the Junction and the Queen Inns also vied with the
shopkeepers in the display of "red, white and blue". Soon after the first train came
up, Mr Edwards, of the firm of Messrs Waller and Co. contractors for the new line,
invited Mr John Hargreaves, the station master; Mr Fielden, engineer; Mr Terry,
travelling inspector and the other officials who had arrived by the train, to lunch at
that well-known hostelry, the Golden Lion, where a substantial spread was offered
by Mrs Dugdale, the hostess. The first train down to Sowerby Bridge was at 9.35,
by which 180 passengers booked. At 10.30 the train again left Sowerby Bridge for
Ripponden, conveying over 100 passengers in eight minutes, reckoning from
platform to platform. Shortly before noon the Rishworth Brass Band made its
appearance, and in their lively uniforms the men paraded the streets, playing
selections of spirited music. Afterwards they marched to the station, proceeding
by train to Sowerby Bridge, and returning by the next train up. The proceedings of
the day commenced as early as half past four, when a merry peal was rung out at
Ripponden Church, the performance on the bells continuing at intervals till nine
o'clock. One of the two cannons was fixed near Height Farm, a point on the side of
the hill overlooking the village from the Barkisland side. The firing, which commenced at half past four and continued at intervals all day, was superintended by
Messrs Booth, Mitchell and Garside. Another cannon was placed in the Holmes,
behind the Waterloo Inn, where Mr Mackerill (the landlord) and others ensured
very loud reports. The majority of the mills closed all day, and the rest only
worked till breakfast time. A large business was done at the public houses and
especially were the Old Bridge Inn (said to be the oldest licenced house in the
parish of Halifax), the Golden Lion, kept by that amiable looking lady, Mrs
Dugdale, and the Queen Inn, centres of attraction, for there some of the oldest
inhabitants of Sowerby Bridge conversed with old acquaintances at Ripponden on
the event of the day, and said "I never expect to see another line opened." Here,
two tradesmen, from Sowerby Bridge, with an eye to business, endeavoured to
cultivate a closer acquaintance with their future customers, and spoke of the
benefits to be expected from the new railway.

A word as to the delay in the construction of the line. Although the Lancashire
and Yorkshire Railway Company obtained powers in 1865 to construct the Ripponden branch railway, it was not convenient to commence the work. In 1869,
notice was given of an application to Parliament for the purpose of extending the
time fixed for the purchase of the land, for the sanction of an extension of the line
as far as Slitheroe, and the abandonment of part of the first scheme. The extension
to Slitheroe makes the line one mile, seven furlongs, and four chains longer, the
first scheme being two miles, seven furlongs, and six chains. In 1870 the application was granted. Operations were not actually commenced till the last week in
August 1873, when a number of men were set to work about the centre of the

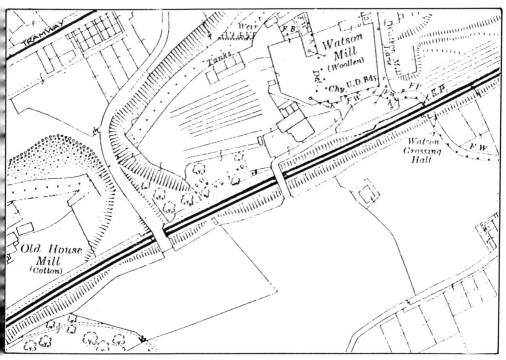

Watson Crossing Halt. Reproduced from the 1919 25″ Ordnance Survey Map.

This photograph appeared in the *Halifax Evening Courier* on the 11th August, 1978 with the following caption. "One hundred years ago this week the little branch railway from Sowerby Bridge to Ripponden, and subsequently to Rishworth, was opened. Closed to passenger traffic in September, goods were carried as far as Ripponden until September 1st, 1958 and this photograph is of the last goods train as it passed Watson Crossing on its way."   *Courtesy, Evening Courier*

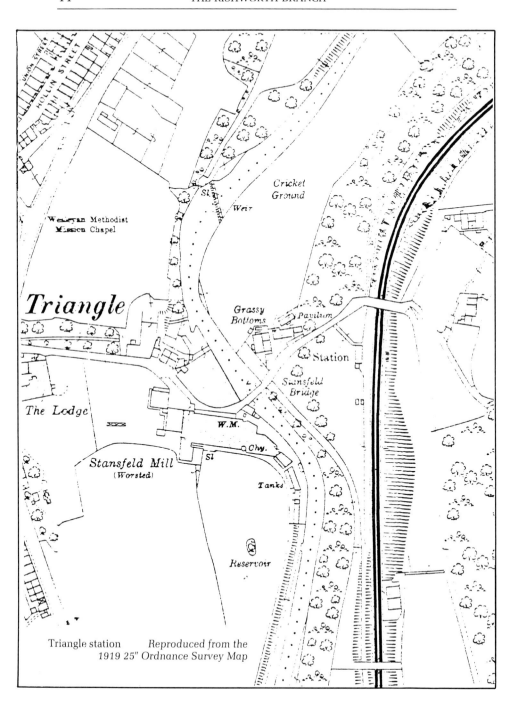

Triangle station   Reproduced from the
        1919 25″ Ordnance Survey Map

proposed line, preparatory to commencing the excavations and the heavy work. Thus it has taken nearly five years to construct a line about four miles long. This has arisen through the great landslips in Rough Hey Wood and at Scar Head. These facts have made the construction of the line a very expensive proceeding. Just behind Kebroyd is a cutting, mostly through solid rock, 350 yds long, and 52 ft deep at the deepest point. Before Ripponden is reached another cutting is passed, 286 yds long, and 33 ft deep at the deepest point. The road from Ripponden to Barkisland is crossed by a bridge of 35 ft span, and 16 ft in height. Going forwards towards Slitheroe is another cutting through the shoulder of the hill, 680 yds long, and 40 ft deep, and a viaduct 150 yds long, and 75 ft in height, crosses the river. The tunnel under Scar Head has also proved a most expensive work. So far, only one station has been erected, viz, at Ripponden, but we believe that steps are being taken shortly for building one at Triangle and another at Slitheroe. The station at Ripponden has a light and airy appearance. It is erected on the Barkisland side of the line, being approached by a flight of steps from the road to Barkisland. The booking office is situated between the general waiting room and the waiting room for ladies.

The plastering and painting of the station was let by the railway company; and was done by Messrs Bancroft and Son, plasterers, Halifax; and Mr Robt Moores, painter, Ripponden. The work reflects credit on both these firms, and the painting is done in very pleasing colours. The goods warehouse and weighing machine are situate behind the passenger station. Although the line has only been open a few weeks for goods traffic, yet it has already been found that there is not sufficient goods accommodation. Perhaps when the Slitheroe station is opened this may be relieved. The effect of the line has already been felt. The road from Sowerby Bridge to Ripponden has almost a deserted appearance, and several farmers in the latter district are selling their horses. The coal business done at Ripponden station has been considerable, and as much as 70 tons of coal being weighed daily. Of late years the business done in Ripponden and the neighbourhood has been largely increased, and especially may this be noted in the cotton business. Bodies of working men have put together their savings, and commenced business as cotton spinners. Beginning in a small way, they have by dint of frugal habits, hard work, and perseverance, succeeded in filling their mills with machinery. In this manner a race of cotton masters has sprung up and employment has been found for the families living in the district. There cannot be much doubt that the new line will further develop trade in the district, especially when the line is continued to Littleborough or Oldham, thus affording a much shorter route between the large towns of Yorkshire and Manchester and Liverpool.

In conclusion we may state that 996 tickets were issued at Ripponden on Monday, and several passengers had to go without tickets, but paid their fare on arriving at Sowerby Bridge. The number of passengers to and from Ripponden were calculated to be upwards of 2,000 on that day. At Sowerby Bridge, the tickets provided for the journey to Ripponden were all used up, and tickets used for Mytholmroyd were used instead. To cover expenses incident to the engagement of the Rishworth Brass Band, which was playing all day on Monday last, and the firing of the cannon, which commenced at early morn, and continued till dark, a subscription was made, and we have to report that after paying all claims, a balance of 15 shillings remained. This sum has been handed to the chairman of the Ripponden Commercial Company for distribution amongst the aged poor of this district.

Though there is a good service of trains to and from Sowerby Bridge, and an extra market train each way on the Saturday, an earlier train than 9.35 from Ripponden for the convenience of tradesmen going to distant towns such as Manchester, Liverpool, Leeds and Bradford, would be an advantage.

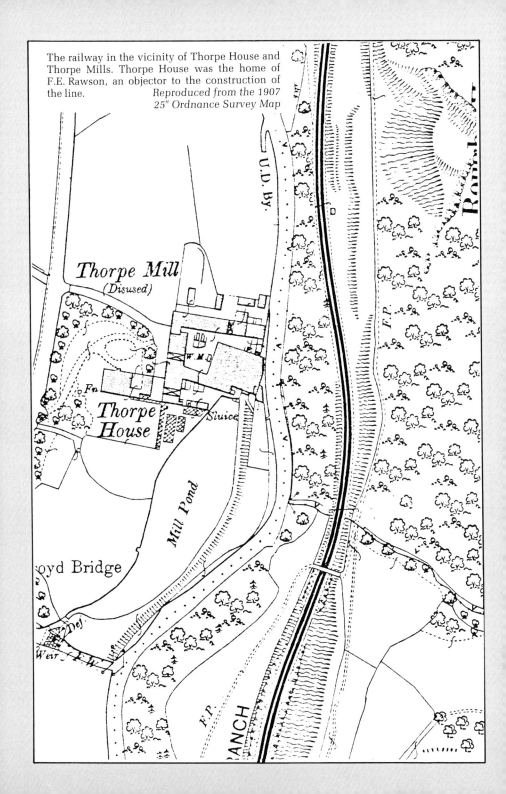

The railway in the vicinity of Thorpe House and Thorpe Mills. Thorpe House was the home of F.E. Rawson, an objector to the construction of the line. *Reproduced from the 1907 25" Ordnance Survey Map*

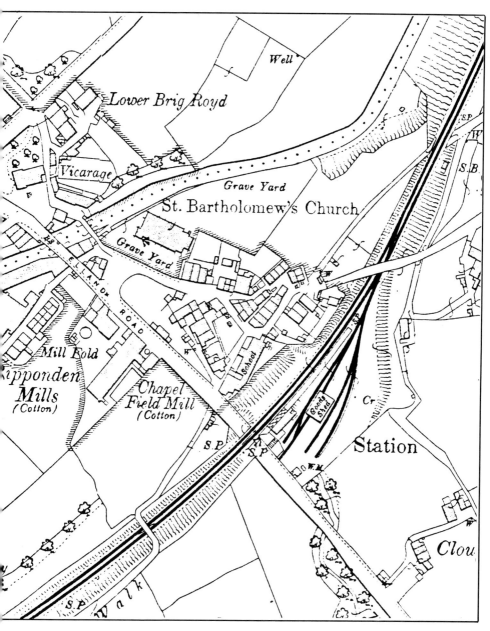

Ripponden station. *Reproduced from the 1907 25″ Ordnance Survey Map*

Although a double track branch it would appear that the station at Ripponden only had one platform. Some records of the line indicate two platforms but in the above article it states the station at Ripponden is erected on the Barkisland side of the line. Additionally a Lancashire and Yorkshire Railway Company plan of the signalling arrangements on the branch dated 13th December, 1883 showed only one platform. This plan also showed that the section between Ripponden and Rishworth was operated as a single line, the up line not being used for running.

It will be noted that reference is still being made to the extension of the line to Littleborough to form an alternative main line. The line was built as double track throughout, which was presumably for this reason, although all the evidence seems to indicate that such a development was always a pretty forlorn hope. One interesting statistic on the opening day is that more passengers were carried than on any other Lancashire and Yorkshire Railway Branch at its official opening. There were a minimum of eight passenger workings each way daily throughout the life of the branch, with initially the first and tea-time workings running to and from Halifax.

The table of fares adopted by the company at the opening was relatively complex, the details being taken from the *Halifax Guardian* of 3rd August, 1878:

single journey to Halifax – first class 1s. 3d.
         second class 11d.
         third class 7d.
         Parliamentary 6½d.
return journey to Halifax – first class 2s. 1d.
         second class 1s. 7d.
         Parliamentary 1s.

Nearly two months after opening local tradesmen and manufacturers were complaining vociferously regarding "the meagre accommodation provided for goods traffic" at Ripponden.

The facilities at the goods yard consisted of four roads, each of them accommodating about eight wagons. The warehouse was constructed to the general plan used by the Lancashire and Yorkshire. It included parallel road and railways going through the building with a central loading platform in between.

Three coalmen used the yard at Ripponden, one of these, the local Co-Operative Society, having its own wagons. The following is an extract from the Lancashire and Yorkshire minute book of 13th March, 1894: "Application received from the Ripponden Co-Operative Society to erect a coal office in the company yard. Considered and ordered to be complied with, a rental of £3 3s. 0d. a year to be charged and an agreement entered into". The two other coalmen to use the yard used colliery wagons, largely from the Barnsley area.

At the time of the opening of the branch the locomotives used were probably based at Halifax shed. This shed was demolished in 1884 to allow for the extension of the station.

Reference is made in the newspaper article recording the opening day to the painting of the station. The following is the Lancashire and Yorkshire specification for painting buildings, taken from the Company's files: "Station buildings and signal cabins will be painted in the Company's standard colours of purple, brown and buff. Interior ironwork, including awnings, etc., should be painted buff; exterior paintwork, bridges, water columns etc. are to be painted black. Wooden structures, platelayers' huts etc. are to be tarred".

An 0–6–0ST, No. 311 seen here in 1911 with a ballast train at Watson Crossing.
R. Dyson Collection

One or Five days at the Sea Side.

RIPPONDEN & DISTRICT SUNDAY SCHOOLS.

22nd ANNUAL EXCURSION.

The Committee have made arrangements with the L. & Y. Ry. Co., to run a Special Fast Excursion Train to

LIVERPOOL

On Friday, Aug. 25th, 1893,

FROM THE FOLLOWING STATIONS :—

RISHWORTH 4-45 a.m., RIPPONDEN 4-50 a.m., TRIANGLE 4-55 a.m., SOWERBY BRIDGE 5-5 a.m.

RETURNING from Liverpool (Exchange Station) 9-30 p.m.

Fares for the Double Journey :— **3/-** Children under Twelve Half-fares.

FIVE DAYS' TICKETS, 4/3.

Very few of our Towns can boast of such varied attractions as Liverpool. In the first place, there are the enormous Docks, along which, there has lately been built the **Electric (Overhead) Railway,** six miles in length. Anyone can spend a very interesting day on the Docks ; the River, crowded with all manner of craft, from a Coal Barge to an Atlantic Liner, is a perfect panorama. Steamers sail regularly up the River Mersey, also to Llandudno and North Wales, passing the Training Ships, to the **Manchester Ship Canal,** at Eastham, the work of the age. There is the **Mersey Tunnel,** one mile in length, which, passes under the bed of the river ; the Tunnel was completed at enormous expense in the Jubilee Year. Besides the Docks, Liverpool is also famous for its splendid Buildings, such as the St. George's Hall, the Walker Art Gallery, the Public Library and Museum, &c., &c. They have moreover, one of the largest and most Picturesque Parks in the United Kingdom, purchased from Lord Sefton, whose name it bears, at a cost of £250,000.

1893 Sunday School Annual Outing for Liverpool from Rishworth. A long day ahead with departure at 4.45 am, but what value at 3 shillings for adults and 1s 6d. for children. *R. Dyson Collection*

Chapter Six
Extension to Rishworth

The Rishworth extension of the railway was not to be opened for a further three years, in 1881, although it would appear from newspaper comments in 1878 that it was largely in place at that time.

Various reasons were put forward for the extension, but it appears that it was mainly intended to provide additional goods handling facilities for Ripponden, providing a cheaper alternative from a construction point of view than enlarging the yard at Ripponden. It may well not have been the original intention to provide a passenger service although this was ultimately the case, thought to be as a result of a local deputation approaching the L & Y Board, the line opening for both passengers and goods on the same day, Tuesday 1st March, 1881.

Perhaps the level of celebration was not quite so intense as with the original opening to Ripponden, but nevertheless it appears to have been quite a day as the *Halifax Guardian* of Saturday 5th March, 1881 faithfully records:

> RISHWORTH EXTENSION OF THE RIPPONDEN RAILWAY – Shrove Tuesday was a day of good rejoicing in Rishworth and neighbourhood, the occasion being the opening of the Rishworth extension of the Ripponden railway. The Act authorising the construction of the line to Slitheroe was obtained on 22nd May, 1865, from the House of Commons, and on June 26th of the same year it passed through the House of Lords. The present extension is the completion of the scheme of the Act then obtained. The first train from Rishworth to Halifax started at 7.40 am and carried several passengers, and the 9.30 was also well filled. By the latter train, the pupils of the Rishworth Grammar School, with their teachers, travelled to Sowerby Bridge, being treated with a return ticket by J.W. Wheelwright Esq, Heathfield, Rishworth, one of the trustees of the school. As the train steamed out of the station, ringing cheers broke forth both at Rishworth and Ripponden, from the passengers and others, who had congregated to witness the event. During the day (the mills being closed in the afternoon) the trains were all well filled, most of the mill hands taking advantage of the opportunity of having a ride on the opening day, the fare, third class, from Ripponden to Rishworth, being only 1d. There are ten trains daily each way between the Slitheroe terminus and Sowerby Bridge.

Rishworth was the smallest of the Lancashire and Yorkshire branch termini in Yorkshire. The station was similar to that at Ripponden. The station buildings were typical of Lancashire and Yorkshire practice at the time, using honey coloured stone, flecked with black. The goods yard had four long sidings, three with a capacity of more than 20 wagons. A bay road and a further goods siding were located behind the station platform. The warehouse had square entrances and windowless side walls, there was a derrick mounted on the warehouse platform for freight transhipment plus a heavy duty crane sited in the yard. The village of Rishworth is located on the opposite side of the valley, access to the station being via a timber bridge, approximately 25 feet high, with a deck width of 20 ft, which was laid with stone setts. Originally there was a signal box at Rishworth. The box was of the early Lancashire and Yorkshire "Cammell" design, named after the firm who designed this and many similar boxes.

Goods traffic was fairly heavy with local industries, including paper-making and cotton. There was also an iron foundry which gave some iron

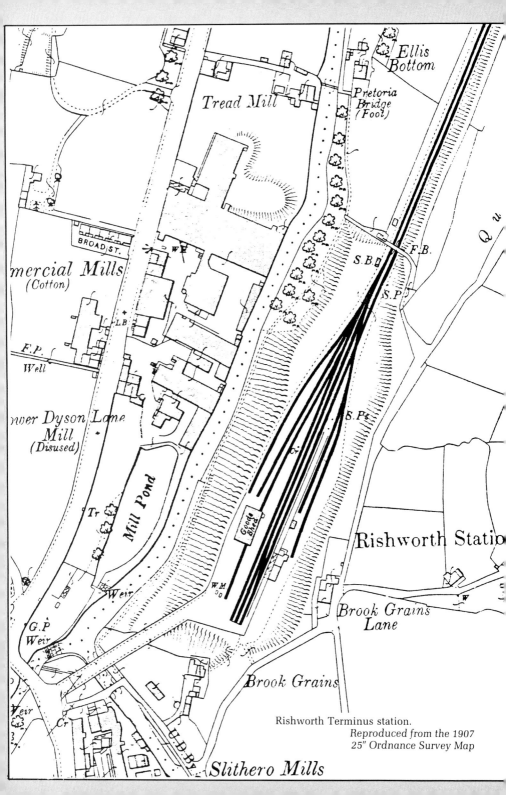

Rishworth Terminus station.
Reproduced from the 1907
25″ Ordnance Survey Map

(Slitheroe)

Station

RISHWORTH TRESTLE BRIDGE
Diagrammatic drawing

River Ryburn

The approach trestle bridge to Rishworth station. This spanned the river and the valley and was the only means of reaching the station. It was built of timber in 1880, strengthened in 1923 and finally demolished in 1953.

R. Dyson Collection

All that remains of the entrance to Triangle station, as seen in 1984. *D. Stubbings*

Thorpe House, once the home of Mr F.E. Rawson, an objector to the construction of the line. Now used as a residential home. *Author*

A beautiful photograph of Rishworth station in the 1920s. There was only one platform and the building was identical to that of Ripponden station. The exit for passengers from the station was at the end of the platform, to the right of the photograph.

R. Dyson Collection

traffic. Two coalmen used the yard but, unlike Ripponden, neither of them owned their own wagons. There was some cattle traffic, although cattle pens were never provided, and, prior to 1914, horse traffic for the local gentry. Parcel traffic was quite heavy, this being catered for by a "tranship" van which traversed the branch daily. In spite of the number of quarries in the area there appears to have been very little stone traffic. There were no locomotive facilities at Rishworth, or on the branch at all, the nearest being at Sowerby Bridge. The Lancashire and Yorkshire did not favour small locomotive depots.

A stone and girder footbridge at the lower end of the station gave an excellent view of the whole station layout. At the time of writing the bridge still exists, but it is in a very poor state of repair.

A view of Ripponden and Barkisland station viewed from the centre of Ripponden. The bridge across the Elland Road can be seen to the right of the station.

R. Dyson Collection

Chapter Seven
Rail Motor Trains are introduced

At last, some 36 years after it was first mooted, the whole length of the railway was open to both passengers and goods traffic. The normal passenger journeys were between Rishworth and Sowerby Bridge with occasional trains continuing on to Halifax. Because of the station layout at Sowerby Bridge it was necessary for Rishworth trains to reverse shortly after leaving the station. The Sowerby Bridge layout was spacious and would have allowed a larger station if ever the through running beyond Rishworth to Littleborough had become a reality.

Although this proposal had appeared aborted some years earlier, the *Railway Times* of 28th October, 1882 published details of a proposed new railway from Leeds to Liverpool by a shorter route than the Lancashire and Yorkshire Railway. This scheme probably stimulated further interest in earlier proposals and a survey was made during the week ending 21st October, 1882. The *Halifax Guardian* of that date gave details of the survey:

> The line was to extend from Rishworth Station up the valley south of Rishworth Moor to a tunnel four miles long under Blackstone Edge emerging near Hollingworth Lake, which it skirted to rejoin the main line near Smithy Bridge, a mile south of Littleborough, thereby reducing the distance from Sowerby Bridge by about five miles.

In some quarters it was felt that the decision not to proceed with this exciting but extensive project was one of the most regrettable in the history of the Lancashire and Yorkshire Railway.

Shortly after opening an extension to the retaining wall at Rishworth Station was found to be necessary and on 4th December, 1883 a tender of £1949 from J.B. Walsh for the work was accepted. Stone from the cutting at Sowerby Bridge was to be quarried for this work. Before completion, however, J.B. Walsh went into liquidation and the work had to be completed by his father, G.B. Walsh.

The only work still not completed from the original proposals was the opening of Triangle Station. The Lancashire and Yorkshire Railway Company had asked the Board of Trade if they must provide signalling at Triangle Station. The Board of Trade replied on 21st December, 1883 saying that Home and Distant signals should be provided in each direction which might be worked from a small two lever apparatus on each platform. It also indicated that runaway points were required on the ascending line but that no block telegraph instruments were required. This view was expressed by Major F. Marindin on behalf of the Board of Trade.

On 30th April, 1885 the Board of Trade appointed Major General Hutchinson as inspecting officer for the new station at Triangle. The opening was sanctioned on 4th May, 1885, subject to:

1. Provision of a clock visible from the line.
2. Provision of a shelter on the up line.
3. Name boards being put up.
4. Relocation of up line distant signal.
5. Correction of the numbering on the levers.

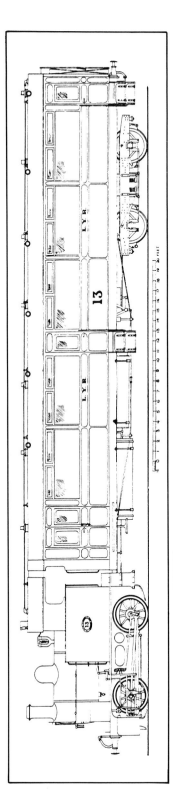

Lancashire and Yorkshire Railway railmotor No. 8.

DIMENSIONS OF THE L&Y RAILMOTOR USED ON THE RISHWORTH BRANCH

Horwich

Boiler:	
Diameter	4' 3"
Length	5' 0"
Centre line	7' 9"
Pressure	180 lbs.
Tubes	191 x 1¾"
Heating surface:	
Tubes	437.5 sq.ft.
Firebox	57.0 sq.ft.
Total	494.5 sq.ft.
Grate area	9.4 sq.ft.
Cylinders	12" x 16"
Wheels, driving	3' 7⅝"
Wheels, trailing	—
Wheels, bogie	3' 7"
Wheelbase, engine	8' 0"
Wheelbase, bogie	8' 0"
Wheelbase, total	54' 8"
Tractive effort	8080 lbs.
Weight (W.O.)	47t. 10c.
Coal	1 ton.
Water	550 gall.
Length over buffers	69' 5"
Length over coach body	47' 6"

The station was opened on 1st June, 1885. The up platform of the station had a wooden building with a brick-built chimney whilst the down platform originally had a shelter. The two platforms were wooden framed, filled with ash and edged with wood. It was situated on a sharp, check-railed curve some one mile twenty-five chains from Sowerby Bridge. Land alongside the station, between the railway and river Ryburn, was purchased for the development of goods facilities but these were never built.

From 1st January, 1892 Ripponden Station was re-named Ripponden and Barkisland, which reflected the fact that the station served reasonably well the adjacent township of Barkisland.

On 16th April, 1894 a new goods outlet was opened at Sowerby Bridge utilising a site in the vicinity of the original passenger station. This was preceded on 20th March, 1894 by a letter from the Lancashire and Yorkshire Railway Company advising the Board of Trade that the works were finished and ready for inspection. Major General Hutchinson was appointed inspecting officer on 22nd March, 1894.

A report by Major General Hutchinson on 7th April, 1894 recommended that the Board of Trade give their approval to the opening of this new goods outlet. It was noted that at that time the tunnel end signal box at Sowerby Bridge, which controlled the goods outlet, had 34 levers of which 11 were spare.

It appears that prior to 1907 most of the passenger services were powered by tank engines, of 0–4–4T wheel arrangement pre-1895, usually with five four-wheeled coaches, and 0–6–2T type post-1895, usually with four six-wheeled coaches. In both combinations one of the coaches would be a first/second composite vehicle. Day to day operation continued in a quiet and successful way, although the justification for construction to main line standards was very questionable in view of the decision not to extend from Rishworth to Littleborough.

Goods traffic formed the main business of the branch. Prior to 1890 this usually consisted of a Hurst 0–6–0 with 10 or 12 mixed wagons and vans. During the period 1890 to 1910 it was likely to be a Barton Wright Ironclad 0–6–0 or 0–6–0ST, also with 10 or 12 mixed wagons and vans. Passenger traffic was not inconsiderable during this period, but one aspect was changing with an increase in competition from road transport, particularly the electric tramway. So far as the Rishworth branch was concerned electric trams only ever penetrated as far as Triangle, but omnibus services were to compete for the remainder of the route. The nearby Lancashire and Yorkshire Railway Branch to Stainland was to suffer more from tramway competition as these vehicles traversed the whole route between Halifax and Stainland.

The Lancashire and Yorkshire Railway Company began working the section of the branch between Ripponden and Rishworth by the electric tablet system on 8th March, 1900. This was in accordance with the rules and regulations approved by the Board of Trade. A plan outlining the proposals was sent by the Lancashire and Yorkshire Railway Company to the Railway Department of the Board of Trade on 26th February, 1900. Colonel Von Donop was appointed to inspect the works. No alterations to the permanent

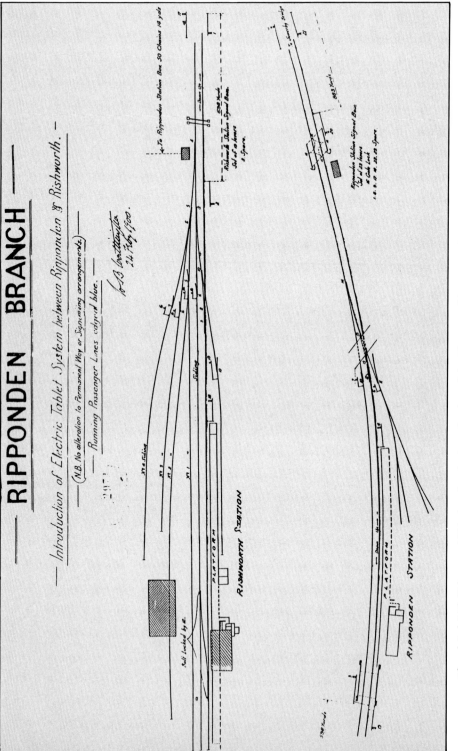

Plan dated 24th February, 1900 showing the introduction of the Electric Tablet System between Ripponden and Rishworth.

Courtesy P.R.O., Kew

A railmotor at Rishworth station. Note in this view, the goods shed on the left and the stone and girder footbridge spanning the line at the signal box end of the station.

R. Dyson Collection

way were involved and all that was required from the Company was an undertaking as to their mode of working.

The following interesting points were noted from the plan mentioned above:

Rishworth signal box had 19 levers, 3 of which were spare.

Ripponden signal box had 23 levers, 7 of which were spare. (The level crossing gate lock was worked by lever 16.)

The distance between Ripponden and Rishworth signal boxes was 50 chains, 14 yards.

In an effort to improve the services on both these branches, in 1907 the LYR decided to introduce a rail motor service which, in addition to being more economical to operate, provided the opportunity for the following improvements:

1. More picking up and setting down points.
2. More frequent service.
3. Better connections with main line trains.
4. Marginally improved journey times.

The last point on the Rishworth branch was due largely to the construction of a new "sleeper built" platform at Sowerby Bridge, thereby avoiding the need for trains to reverse.

The following article from the *Halifax Guardian* of 23rd February, 1907 illustrates the general view in regard to the proposals for both branches:

THE NEW MOTOR TRAIN. Rishworth and Stainland Scheme. There can be no doubting that the intelligence regarding the railway motor-car service for the Rishworth and Stainland districts, which the Lancashire and Yorkshire Railway Company have decided to commence on March 1st next, has been received with much satisfaction by the residents in the districts through which the new service will pass. Not only will the public have a better and more continuous service, with easier methods of reaching the cars than at present, but what is of more importance, the new service has been so arranged that the public will get an excellent connection with the main line and express trains to the large centres. To all, but to businessmen in particular, the newer method is certain to be appreciated. Although the Lancashire and Yorkshire Company have similar services in Lancashire, these are the first introduced into Yorkshire.

Under the present system the number of trains travelling between Halifax and Stainland is ten (each way) per day but when the motor service is instituted, this will be increased to seventeen. The service will practically be continuous from 7 in the morning until 11 in the evening. Some time ago the Greetland District Council wrote the railway company, asking for a roadway to be made from Clayhouse Lane to Greetland Station, but owing to the great cost of such an undertaking, the scheme was not carried out. Now, however, the railway authorities are leaving no ground for complaint on this score, for arrangements are being quickly completed for a halting place in Rochdale Road, with an easy means of access. This will be a welcome innovation, and will "tap" a good district. As is shown on the circulars announcing the new system, tickets will be issued by the conductor to persons joining at the "halt". By this arrangement, the railway company will be an effective competitor for the traffic which the tramways at present enjoy.

With the introduction of the rail motor service on the Rishworth branch line, it has been found necessary to construct a new platform at Sowerby Bridge. Under

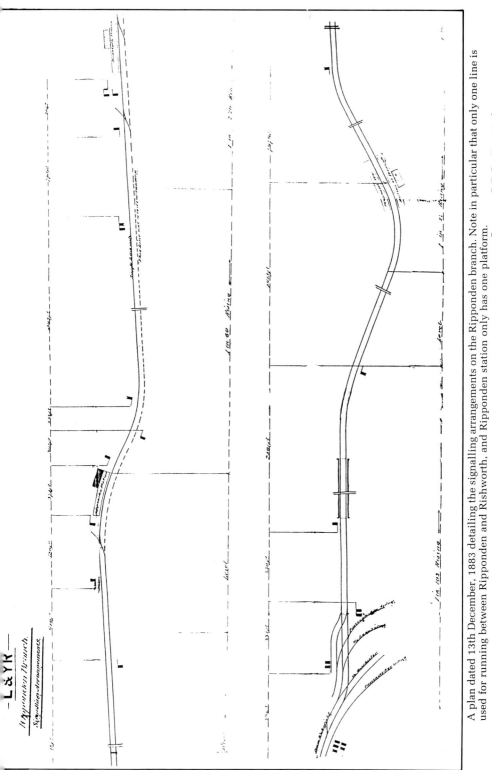

A plan dated 13th December, 1883 detailing the signalling arrangements on the Ripponden branch. Note in particular that only one line is used for running between Ripponden and Rishworth, and Ripponden station only has one platform.

Courtesy P.R.O., Kew; Ref. MT6/396/13

LANCASHIRE & YORKSHIRE RAILWAY TIME TABLES

JULY 1st to SEPTEMBER 30th, 1900.

RISHWORTH, RIPPONDEN, and SOWERBY BRIDGE.

WEEK DAYS.

		a.m.	a.m.	a.m.	p.m.	p.m.	p.m.	p.m.	p.m.	p.m.	p.m.	p.m.		p.m.		p.m.
RISHWORTH	dep	7 50	9 40	10 30	12 20	1 50	3 35	4 35	5 32	6 35	7 40	9 0		9 55		11 12
Ripponden and Barkisland	"	7 52	9 42	10 32	12 22	1 52	3 37	4 37	5 34	6 37	7 42	9 2		9 57		11 14
Triangle	"	7 57	9 47	10 37	12 27	1 57	3 42	4 42	5 39	6 42	7 47	9 7		10 2		11 19
SOWERBY BRIDGE	arr	8 2	9 52	10 42	12 32	2 2	3 47	4 47	5 44	6 47	7 52	9 12		10 7		11 24
Halifax	"	8 26	10 7	10 57	12 51	2 17	4 5	5 3	5 57	8 8	8 9	9 34		10 49		12 2
Bradford (Exchange)	"	8 55	10 37	11 25	1 18	2 47	4 47	5 30	6 27	7 44	8 36	10 0		11 12		12 29
Leeds (Central)	"	9 15	10 44	11 45	1 48	3 20	4 55	5 53	6 45	7 47	9 3	10 10		11 23		12 47
Huddersfield	"	8 46	10 35	11 38	1 20	3 7	4 50	5 40	6 45	7 40	9 12	10 11		12 0		
Wakefield (Kirkgate)	"	8 55	10 45	11 25	1 26	3 30	4 55	5 57	6 37	7 46	9 18	10 32				
Todmorden	"	8A36	10 21	11 20	1 15	2A40	4 14	5 28	6 3	7 39	8A46	9 41		11 15		12 10
Burnley (Manchester Road)	"	8 53	11 0	11 54	2 46	2 59	5 7		6 35	8 51	9 6	10 26				
Blackburn	"	9 30	12 5	1 44	3 15	3 25	5 42		7 5		9 30	11 26				
Manchester (Victoria)	"	9 30	10 53	12 12	1 55	4 3	5 15	6 23	6 43	8 35	9 10	10 35		12 5		12 48
Preston	"	10 20	12 8	1 50	3 20	4 41	6 10		7 54		10 19					
Blackpool (Talbot Road)	"	10C15	12C30	1 C 5	3 30	5B22	6C55		8 32		11C25					
Southport (Chapel Street)	"	11 10	12 10	1 13	3 54	5 34	6 38		7 56		10 23					
Liverpool (Exchange)	"	10 25	12 2	1 8	2 45		6 8	7 15	7 48	9 35	10 13					

Saturdays only. / Saturdays only.

A Stansfield Hall Station.
B Central Station, Blackpool. Passengers arrive at 4-50 p.m. on Saturdays
C Central Station, Blackpool.
* Saturdays only.

SOWERBY BRIDGE, RIPPONDEN, and RISHWORTH.

WEEK DAYS.

		a.m.	a.m.	a.m.	a.m.	a.m.	p.m.	p.m.	p.m.	p.m.	p.m.	p.m.		p.m.		p.m.	
Liverpool (Exchange)	dep			7 55	9 30	11 15	12 30	2 30	3 0	4 7	4 55	6 30		7 30		8 30	
Southport (Chapel Street)	"			8 10	9 0	11 0		2 40	4 3	4 50	5 55		7 10				
Blackpool (Talbot Road)	"			7D25	8D20	10 8	0 10	40	1C27	2D40	3D25	4C30	5 45	7D25			
Preston	"		6E22	8 13	9 2	11	5 11	30	2 15	3 4	4 7	4 40	6 15	7 10		7 44	
Manchester (Victoria)	"	4 55	7 10	9 3	10 25	12 10	1 35	3 25	3 55	5 10	6 5	7 40		8 30		9 25	
Blackburn	"		6E42	8 35	9 15	11 53	13A2	10	4 0	4 37		6 44		7 57			
Burnley (Manchester Road)	"		7E4	9 1	9 44	12 3	12 40	3 14	4 17	5 16	6 52	7 20		8 29		9 37	
Todmorden	"	5 35	7 53	9 47	10 43	12A23	2 27	4 1	4A41	5 47	6 14	8 3		9 15		10 13	
Wakefield (Kirkgate)	"	5 47	7 0	9 31	10 54		1 25	3 30	4 0	5 17	6 15	7 52		8 0		8 47	
Huddersfield	"	5 35	7 47	9 22	10 45	11 27	1 42	3 35	4 20	5 15	6 28	7 50		8 20		8 47	
Leeds (Central)	"	5 0	7 45	9 10	10 15	11 45	1 55	3 0	3 57	5 0	6 0	7 30		8 20		9 0	
Bradford (Exchange)	"	6 15	8 5	9 30	10 12	11 33	2 0	3 10	4 20	5 18	6 25	7 30		8 20		10 35	
Halifax	"	6 43	8 28	9 59	10 49	12 40	2 33	3 43	4 51	5 56	6 56	8 25		9 35		10 55	
SOWERBY BRIDGE	"	7 5	8 46	10 10	11 27	1 0	2 57	4 17	5 5	6 10	7 15	8 40		9 35		10 59	
Triangle	"	7 9	8 50	10 14	11 31	1 4	2 57	4 21	5 9	6 14	7 19	8 44		9 44		11 4	
Ripponden and Barkisland	"	7 14	8 55	10 19	11 36	1 9		4 26	5 14	6 19	7 24	8 49		9 47		11 7	
RISHWORTH	arr	7 18	8 58	10 22	11 40	1 13	3 5	4 29	5 17	6 22	7 27	8 52					

Passengers leave Preston at 5.25, Blackburn at 6-10, and Burnley at 6·48 a.m. on Mondays.

A Stansfield Hall Station.
B Central Station, Blackpool.—Leaves at 10-10 a.m. on Saturdays.
C Central Station, Blackpool.
D Central Station. Blackpool—Passengers can leave Blackpool (Talbot Road) at 8-55 a.m. on Mondays; and Blackpool (Central) at 8-17 a.m. on Saturdays.

The Rishworth Branch timetable for July 1st, 1900. (*See page 66 for Sunday service.*)

Railmotor No. 1 at Watson Crossing halt on its way to Rishworth. Note the new style of coach nameboard on the side of the carriage and not (as previously) on the roof.

R. Dyson Collection

Railmotor No. 12 running in reverse towards Sowerby Bridge seen here at Watson Crossing.

R. Dyson Collection

SOWERBY BRIDGE, RIPPONDEN, and RISHWORTH.

SUNDAYS.

	a.m.	a.m.	p.m.	p.m.	p.m.	
Liverpool (Exchange) ....dep	...	...	...	2 10	5 25	...
Southport (Chapel Street) .... "	...	...	...	2 10	5 40	...
Blackpool (Talbot Road) .... "	...	...	...	1 35	6 A 0	...
Preston .... "	...	7 33	...	2 55	6 40	...
Manchester (Victoria) .... "	...	8 15	...	4 0		...
Blackburn .... "	...	7 55	...	3 37	7 10	...
Burnley (Manchester Road).. "	...	8 42	...	4 20	7 39	...
Todmorden .... "	...	9 20	...	5 3	7B58	...
Wakefield (Kirkgate) .... "	...	9 22	1 38	6 8	...	...
Huddersfield .... "	...	9 40	1 40	6 15	...	...
Leeds (Central) .... "	...	8 55	1 25	5 35	...	...
Bradford (Exchange) .... "	7 0	9 25	1 43	6 5	...	...
Halifax .... "	7 32	9 58	2 22	6 37	8 15	...
SOWERBY BRIDGE .... "	8 5	10 25	2 40	7 5	8 30	...
Triangle .... "	8 9	10 29	2 44	7 9	8 34	...
Ripponden and Barkisland .... "	8 14	10 34	2 49	7 14	8 39	...
RISHWORTH .... arr	8 17	10 37	2 52	7 17	8 42	...

A Central Station, Blackpool.

SUNDAYS.

	a.m.	a.m.	p.m.	p.m.	p.m.	
RISHWORTH ....dep	9 25	11 40	5 10	7 30	8 55	...
Ripponden and Barkisland...... "	9 27	11 42	5 12	7 32	8 57	...
Triangle...................... "	9 32	11 47	5 17	7 37	9 2	...
SOWERBY BRIDGE............ arr	9 37	11 52	5 22	7 42	9 7	...
Halifax .... "	10 2	12 19	5 51	7 58	9 39	...
Bradford (Exchange).......... "	10 35	12 54	6 22	8 55	10 0	...
Leeds (Central) .... "	11 2	1 6	6 55	9 7	10 20	...
Huddersfield.................. "	10 49	12 55	6 30	9 34	10 6	...
Wakefield (Kirkgate).......... "	10 27	12 51	6 6	9 30	10 7	...
Todmorden.................... "	10 43	12 19	7 16	...	10 18	...
Burnley (Manchester Road).. "	...	1 16	8 10	...		...
Blackburn .... "	...	1 58	9 3	...		...
Manchester (Victoria) .... "	11 37	1 0	8 22	...	11 17	...
Preston .... "	...	2 34	9 35	...		...
Blackpool (Talbot Road) ...... "	...	3 39	10 15	...		...
Southport (Chapel Street) ..... "	...	3 15	10 27	...		...
Liverpool (Exchange) .... "	1 38	2 32	10 20	...		...

B Stansfield Hall Station.

July 1st, 1900 (Sunday service). (*See page 64 for Weekday service.*)

Working timetable for the Branch (Weekdays only) for 1921.

WORKING TIMETABLE 1921 (Weekdays Only)

Miles	UP	G	RM	RM	RM		RM	RM	RM	RM	RM	RM	G	RM
	From:	Hfx												
–	Sowerby Bridge	6.30	7.01	7.38	8.11		9.06	10.11	10.42	11.15	12.06	12.55	1.40	2.01
½	Watson Crossing	–	7.03	7.40	8.13		9.08	10.13	10.44	11.17	12.08	12.57		2.03
1½	Triangle	–	7.06	7.43	8.16		9.11	10.16	10.47	11.20	12.11	1.00		2.06
3¼	Ripponden	–	7.11	7.48	8.21		9.16	10.21	10.52	11.25	12.16	1.05	–	2.11
3¾	Rishworth	6.45	7.14	7.51	8.24		9.19	10.24	10.55	11.28	12.18	1.08	1.55	2.14

UP (continued)	RM		RM	E&V	RM	RM	RM		RM	RM		RM	RM
					SX								SO
– Sowerby Bridge	2.48		4.20	5.00	5.19	6.08	7.21		8.26	9.01		9.43	10.55
½ Watson Crossing	2.50		4.22		5.21	6.10	7.23		8.28	9.03		9.45	10.57
1½ Triangle	2.53		4.25		5.24	6.13	7.26		8.31	9.06		9.48	11.00
3¼ Ripponden	2.58		4.30	5.05	5.29	6.18	7.31		8.36	9.11		9.53	11.05
3¾ Rishworth	3.01		4.33		5.32	6.21	7.34		8.39	9.14		9.56	11.08

DOWN	RM	RM	RM	G	RM	RM	RM	RM	RM	RM		RM
– Rishworth	7.16	7.53	8.27	8.30	9.32	10.27	10.58	11.30	12.35	1.12		2.17
½ Ripponden	7.18	7.55	8.29	9.20	9.34	10.29	11.00	11.32	12.37	1.14		2.19
2¼ Triangle	7.23	8.00	8.34		9.39	10.34	11.05	11.37	12.42	1.19		2.24
3¼ Watson Crossing	7.25	8.02	8.36		9.41	10.36	11.07	11.39	12.44	1.21		2.26
3¾ Sowerby Bridge	7.27	8.04	8.38	9.30	9.43	10.38	11.09	11.41	12.46	1.23		2.28
To:				Healey Mills								

DOWN (continued)	RM		RM		RM	RM	RM	G	RM	RM	RM	RM	ECS
						SX		SX	SO				SO
– Rishworth	3.35		4.36		5.35	6.23	7.40	8.00	8.42	9.17	9.19	10.01	11.10
½ Ripponden	3.37		4.38		5.37	6.25	7.42	8.15	8.44	9.19	9.21	10.03	
2¼ Triangle	3.42		4.43		5.42	6.30	7.47		8.49	9.24	9.26	10.08	
3¼ Watson Crossing	3.44		4.45		5.44	6.32	7.49		8.51	9.26	9.28	10.10	
3¾ Sowerby Bridge	3.46		4.47		5.46	6.34	7.51	8.25	8.53	9.28	9.30	10.12	11.20
To:													Low Moor

RM   – Railmotor
G   – Goods Train
E & V   – Engine and Van
SX   – Saturdays excepted
SO   – Saturdays only

the old system it was necessary for the train to "back out" from the platform, but by the newer system this will be obviated. Near to the Sowerby Bridge end of the tunnel the platform will be placed, and here passengers will be picked up and set down again. But this is not all, for an approach is being made dirèct to the covered portion of the main line platform. This will prove a great convenience to the public, for, should it be necessary to re-book, passengers will be able to go to the booking offices at the main entrance to the station. By this means a lot of travelling up and down the steep subways will be avoided. In addition to the present stopping places, a new "halt" has been provided at Watsons Crossing, and here passengers may join and leave the train. Such enterprise as has been shown by the Lancashire and Yorkshire Railway Company in this matter has been certain, we should imagine, to earn its reward.

The motor trains were introduced on the Rishworth branch on Friday 1st March, 1907. The first such vehicles were Kerr Stuart Nos. 1 and 2. They had vacuum operated steps to serve the ground level halt platform at Watson Crossing. These original vehicles were found to be underpowered, and were subsequently replaced by two which were designed by George Hughes and which also had the numbers 1 and 2. The motor trains or rail motors were commonly referred to as the "Rishworth Pig". When the coach half of the unit was leading, the driver controlled the train from the leading compartment, while the fireman remained on the footplate. The new platform built at Sowerby Bridge was constructed of sleepers and located some 12 chains from the junction. It was only the length of one coach, built specifically to accommodate the "motor trains". Watson Crossing halt consisted of a ground level, sleeper-built platform together with a wooden waiting hut. It was located 37 chains from Sowerby Bridge.

From now on the branch was worked as single line, the up line being used as far as Ripponden. The down line was then used for the storage of empty coaches mostly used on excursion trains. A sand drag was provided on the down line at Watson Crossing during the period when that line was used for carriage storage. A space of not less than 30 yards was specified as required between each set of coaches placed on the branch for storage, and the handbrakes had to be padlocked. At Ripponden trains transferred to the former down line, the up line between Ripponden and Rishworth being removed. The down platform at Triangle was also dismantled at this stage. Because of the simpler method of operation, the branch signalling was superseded by the staff and ticket system. The signal box at Rishworth was replaced by a ground frame which controlled only the points for the passenger station and the entrance to the goods shed. The rail motors were shedded at Low Moor.

As a point of interest, the competing electric trams reached Sowerby Bridge in October 1902 and were extended to Triangle in the next two years.

SOWERBY BRIDGE and RISHWORTH (Motor Cars—One class only).—

Up.		Week Days.																					
	Miles	mrn	mrn	mrn	mrn	mrn	mrn	mrn	aft	aft	aft	aft	aft	aft	aft	aft	aft	aft	aft	aft
Sowerby Bridge ¶¶.....dep.	—	7 1	7 38	8 21	9 0	1011	1042	1115	12 6	1 1	2 1	2 48	4 18	5 11	6 12	7 21	8 26	9 1	9 43	1051
Triangle...................	1½	7 6	7 43	8 26	9 5	1016	1047	1120	1211	1	6 2	6 2	53	4 23	5 16	6 17	7 26	8 31	9 6	9 48	1056
Ripponden and Barkisland...	3½	7 11	7 48	8 31	9 10	1021	1052	1125	1216	1 11	2 11	2 58	4 28	5 21	6 22	7 31	8 36	9 11	9 53	11 1
Rishworth ....arr.	3¾	7 14	7 51	8 34	9 13	1024	1055	1128	1219	1 14	2 14	3	1 4	31 5	24 6	25 7	34 8	39 9	14 9	56	11 4

Down.		Week Days.																					
	Miles	mrn	mrn	mrn	mrn	mrn	mrn	mrn	aft	aft	aft	aft	aft	aft	aft	aft	aft	aft	aft	aft
Rishworth................dep.	—	7 20	7 55	8 37	9 35	1027	1058	1130	1235	1 20	2 17	3 35	4 35	5 30	6 30	7 40	8 42	9 17	10 0	11 7
Ripponden and Barkisland...	¼	7 22	7 57	8 39	9 37	1029	11 0	1132	1237	1 22	2 19	3 37	4 37	5 32	6 32	7 42	8 44	9 19	10 2	11 9
Triangle ¶¶.................	2½	7 27	8 2	8 44	9 42	1034	11 5	1137	1242	1 27	2 24	3 42	4 42	5 37	6 37	7 47	8 49	9 24	10 7	1114
Sowerby Bridge 730 ....arr.	3½	7 31	8 6	8 48	9 46	1038	11 9	1141	1246	1 31	2 28	3 46	4 46	5 41	6 41	7 51	8 53	9 28	1011	1118

¶¶ "Halt" at Watson's Crossing, between Sowerby Bridge and Triangle.

Bradshaw's 1922 passenger timetable for the branch.

BETWEEN SOWERBY BRIDGE AND RISHWORTH.

Stabling of coaches:—

The up line between Watson's Mill crossing and Ripponden may be used for stabling empty coaches.

A sand drag is provided at Watson's Mill crossing.

Between Triangle station and Ripponden, rail scotch blocks are provided, and coaches left on that section of the line must be so placed that the leading wheels of the leading coach rest against the scotch block.

Trains left on the section between Watson's Mill and Triangle must be left with a distance of not less than 30 yards between each set of coaches.

The hand brakes at each end of each set of coaches on both sections must be applied fully and secured by chain and padlock.

A supply of chains and padlocks is kept at Sowerby Bridge station.

A competent man from Sowerby Bridge must accompany each train when being stabled on the branch.

Instructions for the storage of coaching stock after the introduction of Motor Trains in 1907. (Note: for the purposes of this book the 'up' line has been taken as from Rishworth to Sowerby bridge, as it was in the 19th century (see plan page 28.)

Single Lines of Railway Worked by only One Engine in Steam or Two or More Engines Coupled Together.—Appendix III. to the Book of Rules and Regulations.

Section of line.	Shape of staff.	Colour of staff.	Staff stations.	Persons appointed to receive staff, and deliver it to, the driver.
Dewsbury (Market Place) Branch..	Round	Black	Headfield Junction..	Signalman.
Huddersfield Branch between Mirfield No. 2 and Huddersfield.	Round	Black	Mirfield No. 2	,,
Silkstone Branch, Darton ..	Round	Red	Silkstone Junction ..	,,
Greetland to Stainland	Round	Black	Greetland No. 2 box	,,
Sowerby Bridge to Rishworth	Round	Black	Sowerby Bridge Station box	,,
Farnley Junction and Farnley Iron Works.	Square	Red	Farnley Junction ..	,,
Birstall Junction and Birstall ..	Round	Red	Birstall Junction ..	,,

Extract from Sectional Appendix, LMS (Central Division) for January 1931.

A special train of 6-wheel stock leaving Scar Head tunnel pulled by a class 'A', Aspinall 0–6–0 locomotive. It is likely that the carriages were being shunted on to the down line for storage, further up the branch. *M. Morris Collection*

Kebroyd cutting between Watson Crossing and Triangle. The check rails on this acute curve can be clearly seen. The bridge over the cutting has gone but the abutments can still be traced. *R. Dyson Collection*

The bricked-up entrance to Scar Head tunnel seen here in 1984. The tunnel entrance on the Sowerby bridge side is almost hidden by a factory and the track bed has been developed as a small industrial estate. *D. Stubbings*

Sowerby Bridge station buildings which now house an engineers' depot. The major part of this building was destroyed by fire in the late 1970s. The area in front of the building is a car park but was formerly an additional platform. *Author*

Chapter Eight
Closure to Passengers

Despite an apparent initial success following the introduction of motor trains, passenger business gradually fell away in the face of increasing competition and the service was to prove relatively short lived. The timetable on page 68, taken from *Bradshaw* dated July 1922, illustrates the level of service.

During the period of motor train operation holiday or "feast" week trains were normally made up of stock which had been stored on the branch during the winter months. Prior to 1925 it would be of 4- or 6- wheeled stock and, after 1925, of low-roofed bogie stock. The introduction of a bus service between Halifax and Rishworth by a private firm in 1926 was to take most of the remaining passengers from the train and a lengthy article in the *Halifax Courier and Guardian* on 15th February, 1929 foretold the end of the passenger service.

RIPPONDEN BRANCH RAILWAY should it be closed for passengers?

Company's proposals.

It has been common knowledge for a considerable time in Sowerby Bridge and Ryburn Valley that the high officials of the LMS Railway Company have had under consideration the question of closing the Ripponden–Rishworth Branch Line for passenger carrying purposes. A decision of that kind cannot be reached lightly for there are many difficulties to be surmounted. An important legal point is involved in the closing of a railway; the comfort and convenience of the travelling public must be considered, especially the contract holders and business men holding traders tickets; and, in this instance, an alternative means of transport will have to be provided. The proposal of the Company is to run a motor bus service between Sowerby Bridge and Rishworth linking up with the trains at Sowerby Bridge. Whether such a service can be arranged, which will adequately meet the needs of the district, and replace the existing train service, is the problem which now appears to be receiving the attention of the officials. A solution of the difficulties had been expected some time but when a *Courier and Guardian* representative enquired this morning the reply was given that no date had yet been fixed for closing the branch line. "No doubt the decision will be announced shortly, but there are one or two difficulties yet to be dealt with", added the official.

CONTEMPLATED BUS SERVICE

It has been pretty obvious for a considerable time that the Ripponden branch line, so far as the passenger service was concerned, cannot possibly be a profitable undertaking. The development of the motor bus services up and down the Valley has drawn the passenger traffic from the railway to the road. In addition to being comfortable the buses run every few minutes and are in touch with the main centres of the population in this area. If the company put on a frequent service of buses they should be able to recapture some of their lost trade.

Many years ago the company introduced what is known as the motor train service, with one class only, and the fare now is 4½d. from Sowerby Bridge to Ripponden and 5d. return. When the line was opened in 1878 the fares were: First Class 7d.; second class 5d.; third class 3½d.; Parliamentary 3d.

Interviewed as to the public feeling towards the company's proposal to close the line to passenger trains, a prominent Ripponden resident, this morning, said he was surprised that the step had not been taken long ago. He held the view that the withdrawing of the motor train might be a little inconvenient for a few people, but if a good motor bus service was put on he believed the majority of Ryburn Valley folk would be quite satisfied. He believed parcel traffic could also be more expeditiously conveyed by the road service.

The passenger service was finally withdrawn on Saturday 6th July, 1929 which meant that passengers had been carried on the branch for little more than 50 years. The last journey on the final Saturday was noteworthy in that the branch train collided at Sowerby Bridge with an engine and van which resulted in the blocking of the main line for several hours.

Watson Crossing halt and Triangle Station were closed completely on withdrawal of the passenger services, but Ripponden and Rishworth were retained for goods traffic. During the period of motor train operation goods trains were pulled by Aspinall 0−6−0s or small-boilered 0−8−0s. Freight traffic was very heavy and trains frequently had to be banked by a second engine. In addition a number of excursion trains continued to operate from time to time. After closure the Triangle Station building was occupied for a number of years as the headquarters of the local scout troop.

A view inside the cab of an Aspinall 0−6−0 No. 52515 with one of the regular Rishworth Branch drivers on the footplate (c.1958).
By kind permission of the Evening Courier, Halifax

Chapter Nine
The Branch is Closed

Goods trains continued to serve Ripponden and Rishworth after 1929 with occasional excursion trains; on 5th May, 1951 the very last passenger train ran on the branch. It was a special organised by the Stephenson and Manchester Locomotive Society pulled by Aspinall 2−4−2T No. 50865. This locomotive was formerly Lancashire and Yorkshire Railway No. 741.

As mentioned earlier in the book, access for the station for road vehicles and passengers at Rishworth was across a wooden trestle bridge. It appears that in the early 1950s the condition of this bridge was giving cause for concern.

As a consequence the closure of the station took place in March, 1952, all services being withdrawn between Ripponden and Rishworth. The following article in the *Halifax Courier and Guardian* on 27th March, 1952 described the situation:

DECAYED BRIDGE COMPELS CLOSURE OF RISHWORTH STATION

The last load of merchandise has been collected and delivered from Rishworth Station. To-day the rail terminus up the Ryburn Valley is a dreary looking spot. The four mile track, which twists and twines up the delightful district from Sowerby Bridge, has been out of action, from a regular passenger train point of view, for more than 20 years, but goods were being worked through to Rishworth up to last week-end.

A warning was given by British Railways, some time ago, that closure of track from Ripponden to Rishworth was contemplated, the reason being that the wooden trestle bridge which connects Rishworth Station with the main road at Slitheroe, and over which all traffic to and from the station must necessarily pass, was no longer considered safe for modern transport.

Since then the structure has gradually deteriorated. The main supporting timbers still appear to be fairly sound, but bits and pieces of the upper part of the bridge have rotted and dropped off into the Valley bottom.

It is deemed a totally uneconomic proposition to embark on the repair work which would be required to make the bridge sound. A final instruction therefore has been issued by the departmental engineers to close the bridge and road.

BARRIER ERECTED

At the main road end, the gate has been fastened and a 10 ft high wooden barrier erected across the entrance. It is not anticipated that the closing of this section of railway will very seriously inconvenience the public. Arrangements have been made for the goods which would normally have been handled at Rishworth to be collected or delivered either from Ripponden Station or from Sowerby Bridge Station.

Everything has now been cleared away from Rishworth. All that remains is an empty platform; derelict waiting room and offices; a deserted warehouse; rusty metals with grass and weeds growing between the sleepers; and broken ramps. The platform and roadside fences are dropping to bits.

END OF SHORT CUT

One result of the closure of the station and bridge will be that people living on the Barkisland side of the valley above the station, will now have no alternative but to use the winding country lane which dips down from the main road, alongside Whiteleys Mill, and crosses the Ryburn stream. Until the last few days these residents, though they had no right of way, have been accustomed to make use of a footpath leading down to the station from the rear and then over the trestle bridge. But the wicket gate has now been permanently fastened.

The above article was accompanied by two photographs, one showing "the deserted station" and one "the trestle bridge, which is no longer traffic worthy".

A photograph in a later edition showing the demolition of the trestle bridge carried the following caption:

Farewell to the trestle bridge which formed the approach to Rishworth Station! Built in 1880/81 entirely of wood, and spanning the Ryburn, the bridge had begun to show signs of decay and its use was entirely abandoned in March last year. Although many of the smaller and narrower pieces of timber are rotting, as demolition proceeds it is being found that a large quantity of the great beams are sound and can be used for other purposes.

After the closure of the Ripponden–Rishworth section of the line the railway continued to operate for a few years, but it seems that the writing was on the wall some time before the total closure took place. Observations by local people during the years 1952 to 1957 noted the following locomotives working on the branch: Nos 52089, 52154, 52179, 52351, 52355, 52400, 52452, 52461, 52515, 52522, 52108, 52411.

The following article appeared in the *Halifax Courier* on 11th April, 1958:

MOVE TO CLOSE RAIL LINE TO RIPPONDEN USED ONLY FOR FREIGHT SINCE 1929

A proposal by the British Transport Commission to close the 80 year old, three mile long railway line between Sowerby Bridge and Ripponden was heard at Ripponden Urban District Council last night.

By closing the line, the estimated annual improvement in revenue will be £2024. In addition, it is estimated there will be a credit of £3000 from recovery of the track.

The branch has been closed to passenger traffic since 1929; being used purely for freight since then. Coal has been the largest source of income, bringing in £2611 in the last twelve months.

ESTIMATED SAVINGS

The Council was told that the only traffic loss envisaged was £250 from coal traffic as a result of lower rates applying to Sowerby Bridge than to Ripponden. Staff saving will be £466, saving on train working £260, and on maintenance and renewal £1548.

Alternative facilities will be provided by road traffic based on Sowerby Bridge; already 85 per cent of the traffic received at Ripponden is dealt with in this way.

When the line closed to passengers in 1929 there was a final journey which was treated as an excursion. After the trip the train was derailed, and crashed into another engine, the line being blocked for eight hours.

The final decision on closure was delayed for a few months after this article but the ultimate fate of the line was announced in a further article which appeared on 14th August, 1958:

CLOSING DOWN

The announcement a few days ago that British Railways intend to close the freight line between Sowerby Bridge and Ripponden has caused a good deal of comment in the area.

Many of the older people feel that the closing of the line from 1st September represents the end of an era, though most of the business men realise that the closing is inevitable on economic grounds.

Some older people have recalled the events of 1929, when the line was closed to passengers. The final journey was treated as an excursion and the people packed the train. After the trip the engine was derailed, crashing into another engine and blocking the line for eight hours.

Mr T.E. Smith, Station Master at Sowerby Bridge, says that nothing has been arranged so far to mark the final freight trip.

Although the train, at the moment, is supposed to run once a day along the three mile stretch of track between the two towns, it often happens that there is not sufficient freight to warrant the journey and the service is cancelled.

The closing of the line will save British Railways over £2000 per year.

And so the final chapter in the history of the railway was about to be written. The closure took place at a time when the railway network throughout the country was being dramatically reduced and there seems to have been no special event or tribute to mark the passing. How different to the opening day.

The following article appeared in the *Halifax Evening Courier* of 30th August, 1958:

END OF A LINE

Another chapter of local railway history closes this week-end. No more goods trains will run up the Ryburn Valley from Sowerby Bridge to Ripponden. The reason for the closing of the line, as we have said, is the heavy financial loss which has been incurred annually.

With the development of road transport the London, Midland and Scottish Railway Company decided to close the line to passenger traffic in 1929. The last train ran on 6th July, 1929. The single coach was well filled and a rousing cheer went up as the train drew out of Sowerby Bridge Station. Passengers joined in the singing of popular hymns and as the train got to the end of its journey "Auld Lang Syne" was sung. At different points from Sowerby Bridge to Rishworth fog signals boomed out. There was keen competition from local people to be the last to leave the train. Some went as far as Rishworth and returned to Ripponden. The affair did not finish in a blaze of glory, however, for when the empty train reached Sowerby Bridge on its return it became derailed and then collided with an engine and a van causing the main line to be blocked for several hours.

The Rishworth extension and the wooden bridge to the station were demolished prior to 1960. The "down" line was removed in 1954, the remainder of the Branch being dismantled and the tunnel entrances bricked up in 1962.

Thus the saga of the Rishworth Railway came to an end after so comparatively short a time. It had served the Valley well particularly in the early years. In spite of the relatively short time since the opening of the line it is difficult to imagine the impact it had, particularly perhaps, with regard to local industry. We do see benefits nowadays from improvements to transport, but the coming of the railway brought the first realistic opportunity for people to travel in speed and comfort some distance from their home towns and villages. This opportunity must have seemed a wonderful, and very obvious, reason for the extravagant celebrations which resulted.

Memories of the railway will not die for a long time yet. The *Evening Courier* carried articles in 1973 to mark the centenary of cutting the first sod, and in 1978 to mark the centenary of the first passenger train to Ripponden.

The remains of the stone and girder footbridge (*see page 61*) which was located at lower end of Rishworth station. Photographed in 1984.   *D. Stubbing*

The remains of Triangle station in 1984, looking towards Sowerby Bridge.
D. Stubbings

Chapter Ten
Postscript

What of the railway since closure? At the time of writing (1988) much of the track bed remains although the majority of the bridges carrying the railway over roads and tracks have been removed. Rishworth Station still exists but in an overgrown and almost impenetrable condition. The platform is very nearly intact but only the foundations of the buildings remain. The cobbled roadway which led onto the access bridge is traceable, as is the extent of the goods shed, although the shed itself is now reduced to a pile of rubble. The footbridge on the Sowerby Bridge side of Rishworth Station also remains but in a dilapidated condition. A depression can be seen near the footbridge where the signal box once stood. In addition a Lancashire and Yorkshire boundary marker is in situ near the bridge.

The trackbed between Rishworth and Ripponden can be walked in spite of being overgrown and, in some parts, very wet due presumably to blocked drains.

Ripponden Station has completely disappeared, the site now being occupied by a small private housing estate. Its former use as a railway is very clear, however, due to the supports for the bridge which carried the railway over Elland Road. Triangle Station remains but, as with Rishworth, the buildings have disappeared. There is only one platform, the second being removed with the introduction of motor trains, and this is in poor condition due to the platform edges being made of wood.

The track bed between Ripponden and Triangle and between Triangle and Watson Crossing can be walked with a number of breaks due to the removal of bridges over tracks. At Watson Crossing the track bed has recently disappeared due to the construction of a new factory. Scar Head tunnel is intact with the entrances bricked up. On the Sowerby Bridge side of the tunnel the track bed is covered by a factory.

Sowerby Bridge Station remains open. It is served by trains between Leeds and Manchester, and Leeds and Blackpool. The station is reduced to two platforms and, since the closure of the remaining goods handling facilities in 1984, all points have been removed leaving just the two lines of rails through the station and alongside the former Rishworth Junction, the goods yard and the engine shed. It has also been unstaffed since 1987 and all tickets now have to be bought on the train. Services have been improved, the Leeds/Manchester service being hourly with many of the trains extending to Liverpool and York or Scarborough. The Blackpool service is two hourly. The railway from Sowerby Bridge to Mirfield through Brighouse also remains open, but for goods traffic only. A loudspeaker system has been introduced for the purpose of advising passengers when trains are cancelled or running more than five minutes late. A fire in the late 1970s resulted in the demolition of the larger part of the station buildings. Some of those remaining are used as a British Rail Engineers depot whilst others are boarded up. An interesting relic is a signal supporting post used for the signal which controlled the Rishworth Junction.

After closure of the railway in 1958 the section of track between Kebroyd and Sowerby Bridge was bought by the then Ripponden Urban District

The former coal-drops at Sowerby Bridge station (now used for building material storage). The main line station can be seen to the left, in the lower photograph. *Author*

Sowerby Bridge station in 1988 with (*top*) a Blackpool train arriving on the right and a York train arriving on the left and (*below*) a Scarborough service leaving on its way to Halifax.   *Author*

Council for £50 and it is now a sanctuary for wild birds.

In 1982 the Chief Town Planning Officer of Calderdale submitted a report to the Development Services Committee on the "Re-use of Disused Railway Lines for Cycle Routes". This proposal included the use of the trackbed of the Rishworth branch and a number of other disused lines in the district. The report indicated that "by linking the railway lines, using canal tow-paths, existing footpaths and mainly quiet, rural roads, it is possible to form a "figure-of-eight" route in the eastern part of the district. This route would be attractive to walkers as well as cyclists and would comply with the Council's Tourism Policy".

The report recommended that it be forwarded to the West Yorkshire County Council and that they be requested to give sympathetic considera-tion to, and investigation of, the Calderdale proposal.

Nothing came of the proposal at that time and the West Yorkshire County Council has subsequently been disbanded. It is understood, however, that Calderdale is still considering the scheme and consequently the Rishworth branch may still have a future as a linear route, albeit not as the original petitioners for the line intended.

An SLS railtour having just arrived at Rishworth in the early 1950s.   *C.J. Gammell*